Design America

CONTENTS

Whether You're a
First-Time Home Builder
or an Experienced Contractor...

...Design America's exceptional home plans and helpful, knowledgeable staff will make your project a complete success!

◆ ◆ ◆

1 Choose the Design America Home Plan Book that offers plans for the style of home you've always wanted.

The plans in our Design America Series have been created by many of the nation's top architects and designers. No matter what your tastes, you're sure to find several homes you would be thrilled to call your own.

You can select from a wide range of styles, including the hottest new trends in contemporary styling. Design America has them all! We also showcase outstanding plans of affordable homes for those who are building on a budget.

In addition to more than 200 home plans included in each Design America book, you'll find a wealth of other helpful information. Companion articles will give you hints on securing construction financing and show you how easy and inexpensive it is to customize your plans.

Order a complete set of blueprints.

Design America plans provide you with a complete blueprint package from as low as **$195.00. Blueprints include the following:**

- Exterior elevations of all sides

- Foundation plans and details

- Scaled floor plans

- Locations of electrical outlets, switches & light fixtures

- Plumbing schematic plan (If available)

- Roof & wall sections

- Cross-section view

- Material list and general notes (If available)

It's reassuring to know that Design America's blueprints meet one or more nationally recognized building standards at the time and place they were drawn. If you'd like a preview of one of our home designs, ask us about a Preview Plan of the home. Some plans offer a Preview Plan that shows the exterior elevation drawings of the plan, the floor plan, and kitchen cabinet elevations.

Customize the blueprints you select for a tailor-made home just for you.

From changing siding material to adding a walk-in closet or a room, our design staff will save you thousands of dollars over what you might otherwise pay. For a nominal charge, we can even mirror-reverse the entire plan!

In addition to design customization, Design America also provides assistance in securing construction financing. **Call us today** and we'll be happy to give you more information on this helpful, time saving service.

Our #1 goal is to help you build the home that matches your needs and lifestyle.

Call us toll free **(800) 533-4350** or fax us your blueprint order today at **(800) 344-4293.** Let's get started on your new home!

Real Life Home-Building Experiences

Are you wondering what it's like to build your own home?

Let those who have gone before you share what they have learned.

◆ ◆ ◆

If you're apprehensive about tackling such a huge project as building your own home (and who wouldn't be?), take heart. People of all levels of experience and backgrounds have successfully built homes for themselves. There are many ways to achieve your goal of a custom-built home. If you wish to avoid as many headaches as possible, hiring an experienced builder to handle all the details is the answer. If you possess a lot of confidence and have the desire to save as much money as possible, acting as your own general contractor is the way to go. There are even those who use a blended approach, hiring a builder to take care of some tasks, and completing the rest themselves. In all cases, the key to success is to do your homework. Doing the proper research first helps to minimize problems down the road. Part of that research is understanding the mistakes others have made so you can learn from them.

Playing the Role of the General Contractor

When you are the general contractor on your home building project, you can expect to have more challenges to deal with than if you hire a builder. Those who have lived through the experience have learned, however, that the snags aren't insurmountable. Sometimes these challenges can be turned into positives and **you can save a lot of money.**

Chuck Weidner, of rural Harvard, Ill. is a repeat customer of National Plan Service USA,Inc. Twenty years ago he used plans from NPS to build a home in suburban Chicago. In April 1993 he and his wife Annette, following a set of Design America plans, started construction on another home situated on ten acres near the Wisconsin state line. They chose the design, a truly grand Victorian home encompassing over 2,500 square feet with an enormous porch that wraps

around more than half of the house. Chuck and Annette are proof that you can play the role of general contractor if you're willing to endure some difficulties. Together, they served as the general contractor on both homes.

Other than five years working in construction (he's a police officer now), Chuck had no experience as a general contractor prior to building the first home. He and Annette taught themselves as they went through the process. What was the most trying part of the whole experience? "Making sure that all the subcontractors got their work done on time," answers Chuck. "Personality conflicts between the subcontractors was the biggest challenge. For example, the carpenters weren't happy with the way the electrician's were doing their work. The sheetrock was delivered at the same same the insulators were here, and it caused some difficulties…you just need to talk to both of them and make some compromises."

Chuck and Annette had the misfortune of buying their lumber shortly after Hurricane Andrew hit southern Florida in the fall of 1992. The demand for lumber for rebuilding caused prices to skyrocket. "The first time we went for bids was in September," explains Chuck, "and then we didn't really finalize it until January or February. The price of just the lumber went up $12,000…that was something we did not plan on."

Despite these problems, work progressed smoothly. The Weidners didn't need to alter their house plans to get the village's approval. There were no construction delays, even for the weather, and the project was completed on schedule. The solution to one particular problem turned out to augment the design of their house. The excavators and laborers were having trouble installing the septic tank because of the slope of the ground. "They had to move the house 15 or 20 feet," explains Chuck, "and that raised the foundation in the back where we now have a walk-out basement."

Chuck & Annette Weidner

Weidner Residence

Photo courtesy of Carl Cullen

When you are your own general contractor, finding a construction loan can also be difficult. Banks are hesitant to lend if an experienced builder isn't involved. "We looked at a few banks," says Chuck, "but they all wanted to see a builder." The Weidners eventually financed the construction of their latest home with a home equity loan taken out on their old house.

"The most enjoyable part of the whole experience was seeing everything coming together," says Chuck, "Towards the end, when all the goodies come in such as the trim, cabinets, and flooring…then it starts looking like a house." Another positive outcome was the money Chuck and Annette saved by not hiring a builder. They **estimate their savings totalled $40,000.**

Would he recommend that anyone try being a general contractor? "I would say yes. With a little guidance from someone that's in the trades who knows what the difficulties are…I think anybody can do it." What advice would he give someone who's considering such an undertaking? "Make sure you're working with reputable people, get several bids, and check with the county where you get your permits, because they can make helpful recommendations (when looking for subcontractors)." Chuck mentioned that negotiation skills are also helpful when dealing with the trades.

Obviously, if asked if they would do it again, Chuck and Annette's answer would be

yes. And, they would use Design America plans. The Weidners were so impressed with the quality of the plans and service they received that they have recommended Design America plans to other people.

Hiring A Builder

Serving as your own general contractor involves managing all aspects of your home-building project. Building materials must be ordered, and competitive bids must be solicited. A complete work schedule must be created, and deliveries and subcontractors' work must be coordinated. In addition, you have to make sure that the subcontractors (or trades as they are also known) get paid on time so that no mechanic's liens are put on your property. Make sure the necessary building permits and insurance are in place, and it's your responsibility that the plans for your house get approved by the village building authority.

If this sounds too overwhelming, consider hiring a local builder to do this work for you. The builder will take care of as much of the project as you want. If you decide to hire a builder, finding a reliable one is essential. How do you go about finding a reputable builder? And what separates the good builders from the bad ones?

"Word of mouth is the best way to find a builder," says Eric Rossi of Avanti Construction Corp., a builder based in the near west suburbs of Chicago. Rossi has been in the business for 20 years and builds 10 to 15 houses per year in Chicago's western and northwestern suburbs. He recently used a set of Design America plans for one of his homes and was very pleased with the result. "Talk to people. See some spec homes. Go in and see the type of work their doing. Talk to people who have bought their homes and ask them what they think of their house," Ross recommends.

There are various third party sources that you can check out as well. Local attorneys and county offices should be able to provide you with information about the track record of a particular builder. Reporting services such as Dun & Bradstreet can be consulted as well. One especially important item to investigate is whether or not the builders pay their subcontractors on schedule. A sub who doesn't get paid on schedule can place a mechanic's lien on your property preventing you from calling it your own until he gets paid. Every builder has had to fend off mechanic's liens at one time or another, however, the fact that a builder has a few doesn't necessarily mean he isn't doing his job. "That's one of the problems in the business," says Rossi. "Any guy that has a dispute can throw a lien on you. There should be some guidelines, there should be some standards that they have to meet, But there's nothing like that." A builder with many liens from several different subs should raise a red flag. A good builder will avoid all but the most frivolous liens. "I don't let things slide. My tradespeople perform and they get paid, and that's important," Rossi states.

It's a good idea to research and hire your builder early, while you're still in the planning stages, and even before your house plans are finalized. This is important because the builder will offer many helpful suggestions concerning the plans and specs. When it comes time to start construction, the builder may know of a more efficient or cost-effective way to achieve a certain result. The builder can also tell you if there are going to be any problems getting the village's approval for the plans. Good builders will always be doing research and attending trade shows to stay informed on the latest issues in the industry. You should tap into this knowledge as early in the process as possible.

Rossi points out that if your home's interior will be completed during the colder months, your labor costs will be less. This is because less construction takes place during the winter and so there are more plumbers, electricians, etc. available. With more trades competing for fewer jobs, they'll be more likely to offer discounted rates during winter.

Builders such as Rossi have built homes for many people and are full of helpful hints. Rossi recommends locating your financing first, before doing anything else. "The first thing to do is to find out what you're qualified for. You don't want to be looking for a $300,000 home if you've only qualified for $170,000. Then your next step is to find your land." Rossi recommends finding a lot in a location you like and then picking out house plans that fit the lot. Don't select your plans before the lot, and allow enough time for construction. "You've got to figure six to eight months to build a house even though everybody wants it in three," says Rossi.

The best piece of advice that Rossi can give to those building their own home is to choose your builder carefully. Shop around and select a builder based on reputation and the quality of their work.

It's Definitely Worth Building Yourself to Get Exactly What You Want.

Having owned half a dozen different houses and condos, Bob and Judy Sipek decided to build a custom home in a southwestern suburb of Chicago. Bob works as a project manager and Judy is a building manager. "We wanted a new home and so we found a lot we really liked in a nice subdivision and started looking for house plans and a builder," explains Bob. "We ended up going with the builder who built my sister's house because I could see he did quality work. I had been talking to various people and had a ballpark figure of what it would cost. This builder's price was in the ballpark. We knew his work and he could start right away so we went with him." In addition, their builder had built other homes in the same subdivision, and was familiar with local building codes and soil conditions.

The Sipeks chose the NP1348 Chesterton design from the Design America series. A contemporary design, the Chesterton features 1,890 square feet of living area neatly packaged into 1 1/2 stories. The home was built on a 1/4 acre lot. "We started looking at

Sipek Residence

plans about one year before we broke ground," says Bob. "The first plans we chose were from a company in Texas. But then we found out that the plans weren't certified for Illinois and it would've been very costly to modify them to comply." The Design America staff was able to deliver plans certified for Illinois and also incorporated some changes the Sipeks wanted to make. Among other things, they enlarged the first-floor master bath and rearranged some closet space to allow a first-floor powder room to become a third full bath. The Sipeks were somewhat pressed for time, but the Design America staff was able to meet their needs. "The company was good at rushing our changes through in about a week," says Bob.

This was Bob and Judy's first attempt at building a home for themselves, and they enjoyed the experience. Their greatest concern was finding a builder they could trust who wouldn't run into financial trouble during construction and be unable to finish. This concern wasn't great enough, however, to cause them to try their hand at being a general contractor.

The only real problem the Sipeks encountered was a time crunch towards the end of the project. There were some rain delays, and a rather complicated roofline took longer to construct than anticipated. Bob and Judy had to wait an extra six weeks to move in, but delays such as these are common. In fact, allowing enough time for construction is one piece of advice the Sipeks offer first-time home builders. They started researching plans and builders about one year in advance of construction, but really could have used a year and a half. It's also important to match the design of your home with your lifestyle. "When you pick out a floor plan, think about how you live," says Judy. "Since we don't have kids, I wanted every place I need most to be on the main floor, and the rooms that we don't use all the time somewhere else. This house fits just perfectly."

Even with the construction delays and minor problems, the Sipeks agree that building their custom home was well worth it. Neighbors are always saying how much they like the house and Bob and Judy couldn't be happier. **"It's definitely worth building yourself to get exactly what you want**," says Judy. "We plan to retire here."

Make Design America Plans Part of Your Home-Building Experience

Many people have built their own custom homes and so can you! Allow enough research time, solicit bids from a variety of builders or subcontractors, insist on quality work, and choose Design America plans. By following these tips from successful home builders, you'll be well on your way to living in that home you've always wanted. Design America also offers books on building and construction to help you start your project with a solid foundation of knowledge. ✍

Analyze the Blueprints Before Building to Create the Best Possible Home of Your Dreams

Article by Guhner-Jahr Publishing
Build-It & Build-It Ultra

There need be nothing "stock" about a custom home built from pre-drawn mail-order plans. In fact, with imagination and/or professional guidance, thousands of homeowners have modified existing blueprints to create truly personal, character-filled homes. Changes can range from simple facade embellishments, such as articulated door and window casings, to major spatial modifications—for example, combining two small bedrooms to create a grand master suite with a bath and dressing room.

Though dramatic in effect, many custom touches may not even require new architectural drawings. Other, more substantial changes are best accomplished with the help of an architect or other design professional, who can prepare any new drawings that are needed.

In either case, it is critical to consider and decide on any changes early in the process, long before construction begins. Otherwise, any bids you solicit prior to changing the plans will be inaccurate. Worse still, if you ask for modifications during construction, your project is likely to be beset by delays and cost over-runs.

Material Choices

Among the simplest changes are those related to materials. Let's say your plans and specifications call for clapboard siding, but you prefer the more rustic look of wood shakes. Simply select the alternative material, change the specification, and you've personalized your home-to-be. Other easy-to-change materials with a potentially big impact on a home's looks include roofing and the trim around windows and doors.

One step further are changes that affect both materials and design. For example, many two-car garages are designed with a single, large door, but you may prefer the lighter look of two single-width doors. Or, instead of the double-hung windows in the plans, you may opt for the more gracious look of floor-to-ceiling casements.

In many instances it's possible to "test" the visual impact of such changes by sketching in the alternate materials on tracing paper laid over the elevations in the blueprints. These changes should not be treated lightly, however, and if you're unsure, it's a good idea to invest in some professional design help. (For more on the importance of material specifications, see "Specifying Your Dream." page 14.)

Floor Plan Changes

Another area to consider is the floor plan itself. Though today's mail-order house plans are generally well-designed with the needs of modern families in mind, it's often possible to make a change or two in the layout that turns an almost-perfect design into an ideal home for your family. Removing a single wall, for example, might create the large, open living room/dining room you desire. Or, raising the garage's walls and roof by just 4 feet could turn an unfinished storage loft into the spacious home office you need.

Kitchens and baths, which are the most complicated and most used rooms in the house, deserve special attention. A luxurious two-person shower, for example, may better suit your lifestyle than a standard tub/shower combination. Similarly, an expanded kitchen

CUSTOMIZE IT !

*Small changes
on paper can
greatly improve
your plans,
but make sure
you decide
on any
modifications
before
construction
begins.*

◆ ◆ ◆

that can accommodate two sinks and dishwasher may be the perfect solution if you entertain frequently.

Again, you can begin by sketching your ideas on tracing paper laid over the blueprints. If you can't figure out the layout changes needed, seek professional advice from an architect or other design professional.

Working with Pros

If you're confident about the changes you desire but can't quite visualize or draw them, you can hire an architectural draftsperson—perhaps a local architecture student—who can turn your ideas into finished plans and/or elevations. Rates for drafting start at about $25 per hour.

If you need design help or advice about materials—especially if you're considering changes that will affect the house's structure, such as moving or removing walls—seek the services of an architect or other qualified design professional. Registered architects are trained to address both spatial and structural questions. Designers vary more in training and experience; some are best at what was traditionally called decorating, while others are fully adept at space planning.

Many architects and designers will work on an hourly consulting basis, with fees ranging from about $75 to $125 per hour or more, depending on professional accreditation, experience and location.

Kitchen and Bath Specialists

Kitchens and baths are highly specialized design areas, so make sure whatever type of design pro you choose has a lot of experience. One option is to seek out a Certified Kitchen Designer (CKD) or Certified Bath Designer (CBD). To earn this title, professionals must meet special requirements, pass tests and obtain certification from the licensing arm of the National Kitchen & Bath Association

(NKBA). In addition to providing design services, CKDs and CBDs can help you select and can provide materials and products for the kitchen and bath.

Kitchen and bath dealers, many of whom are NKBA members, work out of showrooms that sell cabinets, appliances, bath fixtures and more. Most dealers provide design services and provide products and materials.

A Custom Home Doesn't Have to be Expensive

It's true. If you're planning on building your next home, it's cheaper to customize your own design and hire your own builder than it is to choose a plan from a large developer who's building a subdivision. Even if you accept the developer's stock plans with no modifications, it will still cost you more than building a custom home from your own plans. And the home need not be large, either. No matter if your dream is for 1300 or 3000 square feet, you'll spend less by designing and building yourself.

Why it Makes Sense to Build Your Own Custom Home

You might be thinking, "But how can that be? Can't those big developers build houses cheaper because of the volume of business they do? Don't they get volume discounts on their building materials?" That might be the case, but they also incur significant costs associated with marketing their developments.

It's easy to see these marketing expenses when you take a look at a new subdivision. Consider the model homes that are built for prospective home buyers to tour. The developer has to pay for the interior designers who decorate the homes as well as for all the custom furnishings and landscaping. The salespeople who work there seven days a week must also be paid. Costly brochures promoting the subdivision must be created, and advertising space in newspapers and on television and radio must be purchased. The developer can recoup some of these expenses when the models are sold, but not all of them because the models are sold at a discount. Much of the cost gets passed on to you, the buyer, making the homes more expensive. By building yourself, using custom plans, you can avoid paying those extra costs and have a more personalized home, too!

What's the Best Source for Customized Plans?

You could hire an architect to draw up your custom plans, but you may end up spending thousands of dollars to get the design you want. A better alternative is to purchase customized plans from Design America and spend only hundreds. Design America has top-quality plans, and the expertise and the willingness to back them up with good customer service. Since we've been designing people's dreams for over 80 years, we know what you're looking for in a home. And because of the volume of our business, we can offer customized plans at prices that are 25 – 50% less than what a professional designer would charge.

Example of plan modification

Please Modify to A 3 car garage w/ dormer

3 car garage

Rendering courtesy of Select Home Designs   FIG 1

Even if your future home is less than a mansion, you'll save money by building yourself with custom plans from Design America

◆ ◆ ◆

Revised Plans after modifications

Photo courtesy of Select Home Designs

The Customization Process

The first step is to browse through our Design America Series and select the design that comes closest to your idea of a perfect home. Design America has hundreds of different designs to choose from. If the simplified drawings and renderings in our plan books give you enough information, then fax us your request for changes. Just let us know what changes you need as outlined preceeding page (pg.11, fig.1) and our architects will do the rest.

If you'd like to buy a set of plans first, Design America's helpful design staff will discuss any customization options with you at the time of your order. Feel free to ask as many questions as you like. If changes are necessary, you can tell us at the time of your order. Preferably, you should give us the modifications in writing via mail or fax so there is no confusion over any of the details.

Other home plan companies may ask you to mark up a diagram of the home with the desired changes. But NPS believes you shouldn't have to worry about drawing your plans yourself. After all, we're the architects! We'll do the sketching; you just tell us what you want changed. After we evaluate your request, we'll estimate how much the changes will cost **free** of charge and how long they will take. Of course, price and lead time will vary depending on the extent of the modifications.

NPS Can Provide Your Plans in Several Different Formats

If you won't be making any changes to the stock plans you've selected, then you should order your plans in the form of blueprints. Blueprints are non-erasable and non-reproducible so not even minor changes can be made to them by you or your builder. Order these only if you're sure nothing else will be altered. You'll probably need 4 – 7sets for everyone involved in the construction of your new home. You'll want one set for yourself, of course. The village or local government body that's responsible for approving the design will need a set. Your lender will request plans before a loan is approved, and finally, the general contractor will probably need several sets for all of the subcontractors.

If you want to make only very minor changes, ones the contractors can make themselves, then you should order plans that are reproducible. These plans can be erased and redrawn. If you only want to move a wall a few feet or enlarge a walk-in closet, these plans allow the contractor to erase lines and redraw them. Mylar, vellum plans are also reproducible, so you can make as many copies as you need for all the parties involved. Because mylar, vellum plans are reproducible, they are slightly more expensive than blueprints.

The Design America Advantage:

Other home plan companies' service will stop after you've received your modifications of the plans. They'll redraw the plans and send them off to you. But what happens if the village authorities won't approve construction because your plans don't meet local codes or ordinances? This can be a serious problem. And the fewer problems you have when building a house, the better. What good are plans for a home that can never be built? With other plan companies, you're on your own, but not with Design America.

We realize that local building codes may be complex. Our plans are drawn to meet one or more national standards. Sometimes this isn't enough, however. Regional and local authorities often have their own sets of codes that must be met. If you're building in a subdivision, the seller of the lots may impose certain building restrictions or covenants that must be followed. In some cases, you may not fully understand the codes, or some restrictions may get missed. Design America will help you wade through all of this bureaucracy and help you get your plans approved.

"We realize that the homeowner may not be well versed on the technical aspects of dealing with all of the different codes and ordinances," says David Azran, President of National Plan Service USA, Inc. "We see ourselves as being a liaison between the homeowner and the builder. If permitted, we'll actually sit down with the homeowner and builder and discuss what has to be done to get the plans approved." If your plans are questioned by village authorities because of code requirements, Design America will get in touch with the village and find out exactly which parts of the plans need clarification. Then we discuss what must be done with you and make the changes needed to earn the village's approval.

One of Design America's customers recently learned the value of this **exceptional service** when a conflict arose concerning the topography of the customer's lot. The local authorities rejected the homeowner's plans because the village felt the home's design was not compatible with a small hill on the site. The builder contended there was no hill, but the village insisted there was. After numerous discussions with the builder and the village, Design America discovered the problem. The village was using out-of-date drawings, and there really was no hill!

Peace of Mind With Your Customized Plans

We're sure you can see the value of Design America's services. This peace of mind is included in the price you pay for your customized plans. So call Design America today, at **(800) 533-4350** and let us assist you in the construction of your new home.

The More Active Your Role in Selecting Materials, Products and Techniques, the Better Your Home

Article by Guhner-Jahr Publishing
Build-It & Build-It Ultra

The best custom homes are carefully tailored to meet their owners' needs and wishes, and nowhere is this more important than in the selection of products, materials and construction techniques. After the workmen leave and you move in, the home will be a complete success only if you're pleased with the wood, glass, metal and stone used to transform your blueprints into a house.

Of course, many of the physical elements that comprise a home are spelled out in floor plans, elevations and allied documents. But some of these specifications may be generic, meaning there are still decisions to make. And even when a specific item is listed, you may prefer a different option—perhaps in-floor radiant heating rather than the forced hot-air furnace shown in the blueprints, or oak interior doors instead of pine.

Though it may seem easier to leave all these details to the contractor, the fact remains that you will live with the results, maybe for a lifetime. So the investment you make now in learning about the options will pay handsome dividends for years. Here's what to consider and how to find information and assistance.

Upgrade from plastic laminate to granite kitchen counters, for example, and your house may cost $7,500 more. Specify floor-to-ceiling ceramic tile in the baths instead of small tiled areas around the tub, and the additional cost might be $3,000 – $5,000, depending on the specific tile you choose.

Naturally, your total budget for the construction of the house will help to determine your material and product selections. The important point is to consider the many options—and their costs—early in the planning stages, ideally before putting your plans out to bid. That way the fixed price you contract for will reflect the many materials, products and techniques you want for the home, rather than choices the contractor may have made to save time and increase his profit.

If you're ready to solicit bids, but haven't made final decisions on every material, tell the contractors to exclude those elements from their prices. Or, if you have a good idea of what you're willing to spend on, say, flooring, ask them to include a flooring allowance of that dollar amount.

Dollars and Sense

One of the best reasons to take an active role in product and material specification is to maintain budgetary control over your project. Obviously, the various options in each product category related to the home carry widely differing price tags, and those costs go directly to your home's bottom line.

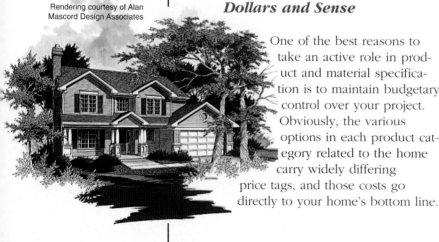

Rendering courtesy of Alan Mascord Design Associates

Rendering courtesy of Alan
Mascord Design Associates

Filling in the Blanks

Another key concern is to fill in the blanks on all specifications that are treated generically in your plans. Though a complete set of blueprints, materials lists and specification sheets represents a comprehensive set of instructions for building a home, it does not necessarily provide a single choice for every detail.

For example, plans may call for "hardwood flooring" without indicating the type of wood or pattern to use. Or they may indicate the size and position of appliances and plumbing fixtures, but not the brands or model numbers. The same may be true of siding, roofing, windows, heating and cooling equipment, cabinetry, door hardware, even such final details as switchplates. In the end, someone must make the decision between inexpensive knotty pine clapboard and top-quality cedar, or between brand X appliances in black versus brand Y finished in stainless steel. And, taken together, these choices will have a profound impact on what becomes your home. Rather than accept someone else's choice, consider the options available in each instance and select the one that best satisfies your needs, desires and budget.

Upgrades

Even when items are listed specifically in the plans, it's worth analyzing the choices and considering upgrades. In roofing, for example, premium asphalt shingles not only look better than standard products, but also carry 50 percent longer warranties, making them a good value over time. Energy-efficient high-performance window glazing offers similar benefits when life cycle costs are factored in, as do top-quality cabinets built to last for decades.

Other changes relate more to aesthetics, but are just as valid. If you've always wanted goldplated bath fittings, why pay for chrome-plated models? Likewise, if standard-issue oak strip flooring is not your dream for a living room, it makes little sense to pay for it now only to switch to polished maple in a few years. Want classic ceramic mosaics on the bathroom walls? Specify them now rather than remodeling later.

Construction Techniques

The techniques used by a contractor to build your home can greatly affect its quality and the amount of maintenance and repairs you'll face over the years. Though your selection of an experienced, competent builder takes care of much of this question, there are some details worth specifying if you want top quality. Here are some important ones that may or may not be listed in your existing spec sheets:

• Drywall should be affixed with screws, rather than nails, which are more likely to pop. Skim coating all ceiling and wall surfaces

with joint compound produces a better looking, more plaster-like finish than simply taping the joints between drywall sheets.

• Vapor barriers should be affixed to studs and joists prior to drywall to prevent condensation in wall cavities.

Rendering courtesy of Alan Mascord Design Associates

• An airspace should be left between insulation and roof sheathing so that air can pass freely from eave to roof vents.

• Sills, the horizontal wood members on top of foundation walls, should be cut from pressure-treated lumber so you'll never have to worry about rot.

• Valleys, rakes and eaves—the most vulnerable parts of a roof— should have a waterproof membrane applied under flashing or shingles.

• Wood siding and exterior trim that will be painted should be back primed prior to installation; this will extend the life of a paint job.

• Interior and exterior painting should include a primer and two finish coats, which can outlast a single coat by as much as 50 percent.

Information and Assistance

The specification of products, materials and techniques is a complicated business. But the task becomes much easier if you familiarize yourself with the available options.

You should also shop local lumberyards, home centers, kitchen and bath dealers, lighting stores, etc., to see and price the possibilities. Collect manufacturers' product litera-

ture and scour design magazines for ideas as well. If it's a book you're after, we recommend "The Apple Corps Guide to the Well-Built House," by Jim Locke, Houghton Mifflin, 1988.

If you'd rather spend your money than your time, consider an architect or other design professional on a consulting basis. Working from your budget and preferences, a pro can prepare a detailed spec list for your approval, can analyze a list you've prepared and suggest worthwhile changes, or can present you with a range of good options.

However you proceed, if your aim is the best, most personal custom home possible, make sure work doesn't begin until there's a complete materials list and specification sheet that you understand and with which you're comfortable. Otherwise, you may have to start planning a remodeling soon after you move in.

Financing the Construction of your Custom Home

by Kevin D. Woodard

Even before you have finalized the plans and site for your new custom home, your thoughts should turn to answering the question, "Where am I going to get the money to fund construction?" Unless you have large sums of cash saved up, you will need to take out some sort of loan to allow construction to begin. A conventional mortgage loan is not the answer at this stage, because you don't yet have a house to mortgage. For some, a home equity line of credit on their existing house can provide the cash they need. For most people wanting to build their own home, however, a *construction loan* is necessary. A permanent mortgage (also known as an *end loan* or *take-out loan*) will come later. This may sound unfamiliar to you, so let's go through the loan acquisition process one step at a time.

1. Select the source of financing

Professionals in the lending industry suggest looking to your current bank first for construction financing. You and your bank are familiar with each other, and the loan officers might already have a good idea of your present financial condition. Banks love to have multiple deposit and lending relationships with their customers and that is a good bargaining chip to have when you are negotiating the terms of your loan. But be forewarned: most banks will not lend to you if you are acting as your own general contractor unless that is how you make your living. Experience in the construction business is everything from the bank's point of view, so plan on hiring an experienced builder to oversee the construction for you unless you have a proven track record as a general contractor.

Other financial institutions can serve as funding sources as well. These include mortgage banks and brokers, and your company pension or savings plan. Retirement plans are often good for providing construction money because of the favorable terms at which you can borrow against your accumulated funds. Another source of funding is the builder himself. Your builder has a revolving line of credit with his bank and can use that to finance the construction of your new home. This arrangement simplifies things because you don't have to go to the trouble of applying for a loan at a bank. But there are disadvantages. A large deposit will be required up front and the interest the builder pays on his credit line will, of course, be passed on to you. You would pay this interest yourself anyway if you were borrowing directly from the bank, but then you would get the benefit of a tax deduction. When looking for possible sources of financing, rely on those who really know the business. Ask real estate attorneys, realtors, and local builders if they can recommend a lender.

2. Determine the type of loan that is best for you

Construction loan plus end loan. This is the most common way to finance the construction of a new home. With this arrangement, you actually get two separate loans to cover your financing needs: one for the construction phase and one for the "live in" phase after the home is built. The construction loan finances all costs associated with

Photo courtesy of Design Basics, Inc.

Photo
courtesy
of Select
Home Designs

building the house. The end loan is nothing more than a conventional mortgage that pays off the construction loan. The construction loan typically has a term of six months to a year and is an "interest only" loan. This means your monthly loan payments include only interest calculated on the amount that you have borrowed. None of your payment goes toward reducing the principal balance. The principal balance is never reduced during the entire term of the construction loan. The interest rate you pay is usually tied to the prime rate and is stated as so many points over prime. The "spread" over prime can be anywhere from 1 to 2 percentage points. The rate will fluctuate as the prime rate fluctuates and may adjust monthly or even daily. Make sure you understand exactly how and on what amount the interest is calculated.

As described below, the loan proceeds are metered out in stages. It's obviously better for the interest payments to be calculated on only that portion of the loan amount that has actually been disbursed. You don't want to pay interest on money that is not even being used yet.

Expect to pay some points when you close on your construction loan. Points are a percentage of the loan amount that must be paid up front. One point equals 1 percent. For example, a one point fee on a $100,000 loan would be $1,000. The lender charges points to cover various expenses associated with administering the loan. It's important to note that these points are not like the optional discount points you can pay on a conventional mortgage. Points on a construction loan are a pure fee for the lender and do nothing to reduce your interest rate. They typically range from 1 to 2.5 points. More points are charged on construction loans than on mortgages, because construction loans are more costly to administer. As an incentive to

stay with the same lender for your permanent mortgage, some institutions will let you use .5 point as a credit towards any points you pay on the mortgage.

A down payment will, of course, be required. Lenders usually require at least 20 percent down. This equates to a loan-to-value ratio (LTV) of 80 percent. Don't expect to get your entire loan amount disbursed to you all at once. In fact, you won't actually see any of the money at all unless you are acting as your own general contractor. The funds will be distributed to the general contractor in increments called "draws." The institution advances each draw when a specified stage of construction has been completed. For example, money will be advanced when the foundation is laid and when the framing goes up. A title company usually takes care of the actual disbursements. A representative of the lender or title company will usually inspect the project before each draw to verify that the work is being completed as planned. In addition, you the borrower may be required to sign off on each completed stage before a draw is made.

After the construction phase, when your new home is ready to be occupied, you're ready to take out the end loan. The end loan can come from the same lender as the construction loan or from a different lender.

Combination loan. Unlike the scenario presented above, in this case one loan takes care of all the financing. At the end of construction, the construction loan is simply converted into a permanent mortgage. This can save you money on closing costs since you only have to close once. Of course, you must use the same institution for construction and permanent financing.

Home equity loan. If there is a lot of equity built up in your present house, a home equity line of credit could be used as a construction loan. Equity credit lines usually have minimal paperwork and lower costs associated with them. Up to 80 percent of your home's market value may be available to use for construction financing.

3. Gather information and documents required at the time of the loan application

Here is a list of items that lenders typically require you to provide at the time you fill out a loan application:

Sworn contractor's statement. This document itemizes the contractor's estimate of all costs associated with building your home. It also lists who the subcontractors are and what they will do. It is signed by the general contractor.

General contractor's information letter. This is a form that the lender asks the builder to complete. It asks the general contractor questions about experience, insurance, bonding, etc. It helps the lender evaluate the general contractor.

Detailed blueprints and specs. The bank or other lending institution doesn't want to lend more than about 80 percent of the estimated value of the completed home. Blueprints and specs are needed for making this estimate of market value.

Signed contract between the builder and the individual. This proves you have an experienced builder working for you. It also assures the lender that the house will be built.

Deed to your lot. The lender will not grant you a loan without first knowing that you own the land on which your home will be built. If the lot is mortgaged, you will also need to have on hand all of the relevant loan documents.

Personal financial information. These are the standard items commonly required by all mortgage lenders and serve to verify your income, expenses, assets and liabilities. You'll be required to provide W-2s, paystubs, previous addresses for the past two years, name and address of employer, information on bank accounts, and outstanding loan balances, etc.

4. Close on the loan and start construction

Just as in a closing for a permanent mortgage, there are costs associated with closing on a construction loan. In addition to the points mentioned earlier, there will be recording fees, attorneys' fees, notary fees, etc. Costs such as these can vary from lender to lender, so it's a good idea to compare points and fees when shopping for a construction loan.

It's a lot of work finding construction financing and evaluating all of the options. But it will all be worth it as you watch your custom home take shape.

To help you evaluate your different financing options, Design America now offers a financing referral service. Call Design America today at **(800) 533-4350** to find out more about this new time-saving service.

Photo courtesy of
Select Home Designs

A Wealth of Information When You Decide To Build Your Own Home

Now that you've decided to build your own home and have picked the plans ...where do you go? With today's home improvement market booming, you, the consumer, have more choices then ever before. Below are some helpful hints.

LUMBER YARDS

Materials, materials, materials ..How much do I need? ...How much will they cost?...What grade of lumber should I purchase? **Your local lumber dealer is the place to start.** Here you will find a service or lumber desk. The people behind that counter just may be your next best friends. You'll typically find estimators on hand who can provide a "take off", in other words an estimate, from your blueprint or materials list. This will be based on the grade of materials that you specify. Their estimates are typically right on target. Remember that they are in the business of selling lumber. Thus you will find them both helpful and attentive because they want your business.

Although don't expect them to do it while you wait; they usually are working on numerous sets at any given time. This is especially true in early and middle spring when the majority of housing starts take place.

HOME CENTERS

Huge stores, miles of products, and helpful staffs. Although you may be overwhelmed by its sheer size you can find practically anything here. Today's typical home centers can be over 100,000 square feet with full service garden building centers. Here you get both discounted prices and idea centers. These stores have everything for home improvement and more.

You ramble past full kitchen and bath displays, order custom blinds, browse through thousands of different wall paper patterns and borders.

HARDWARE STORES

Here is the place to go when things get down to the nitty gritty or you need speed and convenience. When your stuck on a pipe fitting or need specialized fasteners your local hardware store will help you. Hardware store are the one retail outlet where a local and community atmosphere exists. Employees here will help you answer the most difficult questions and help you find the most distinguished nuts and bolts.

A Quick Guide so You'll Know What to Expect Once Construction Begin

Now that you've settled on your plans, the joy of turning your dreams into reality begins in earnest. The wrenching matter of financing needs to be settled, and a patch of land selected. Such decisions can take weeks or even years, depending on your determination and sometimes your luck. But once the time comes to break ground, a house can't be built fast enough.

Constructing a home can take anywhere from six months to one year (or more), depending on a number of factors. The size of the house, number of workers, weather conditions and unexpected—but inevitable—delays, all make a difference. Though the order of work may vary slightly and local building inspection requirements differ, this timetable, spread over a seven-month period, will give you a sense of what to expect and when.

Rendering courtesy of
Alan Mascord Associates

Months 1 & 2

- Municipal and state permits obtained
- Site work and excavation
- Pour foundation
- Building inspection of foundation
- Frame floors
- Rough-in electrical and plumbing under floors
- Inspection of rough-in mechanical systems if house is built on slab
- Install first floor subfloor

Months 2 & 3

- Frame walls, roof and ceilings, including all door and window rough openings
- Install remaining subfloors
- Apply exterior wall and roof sheathing
- Rough-in remaining electrical and plumbing lines in wall, ceiling and floor cavities.

Months 3 & 4

- Building inspection of mechanical rough in and exposed structural work
- Apply roof flashing and shingles or other roofing material
- Install windows and exterior doors
- Apply exterior trim (window and door casings, fascia)
- Apply exterior wall finish material (i.e., clapboard, vinyl siding, stucco)

Months 5 & 6

- Install cabinets and countertops
- Apply ceramic tile in baths
- Finish plumbing and electrical work (light switches and fixtures, outlets, install sinks, tubs, etc.)
- Painting and wallpapering
- Install finish flooring

Months 6 & 7

- Install appliances
- Install hardware
- Inspection by homeowner and final touch-up work
- Site cleanup and landscaping
- Final building inspection
- Final payment to contractor
- Move in!

*Article Courtesy of
Guhner-Jahr USA Publishing*

Design America Designers

National Plan Service USA, Inc.
(The publisher of the "Design America" house plan book series)

With a history that dates back to the early 1900's, when it offered do-it-yourself plans to lumber dealers, and individual consumers, the motto of National Plan Service USA, Inc., has become "Turning Your Dreams Into Reality For Over 80 Years."

Based in Bensenville, IL, the in-house staff of registered architects and designers at NPS work to provide consumers with unlimited design possibilities. These designs range from starter homes to luxury designs, with many alternatives to fit virtually any home-building budget. Home plans from NPS can easily be modified to suit a buyer's particular needs and lifestyle. The company offers customization services, as well as general advice and assistance to make the experience of building a new home as pleasurable as possible.

Many NPS designs reflect the regional influences of the northeast and midwestern United States. These solid, time-proven designs incorporate feedback from the thousands of customers who now live in homes built from fully detailed blueprint packages provided by NPS.

DESIGN BASICS, Inc.

Design Basics, Inc. creates home plans for builders nationwide. The company markets its plans, which are designed for single family dwellings, through catalogs and trade publications. The company originated in 1983 when its primary purpose was to design plans for custom home builders in the metropolitan areas. Seeing danger in controlling too much of the local market, the company's focus shifted from designing custom home plans locally to designing plans that were adaptable anywhere. Included in these plans is a construction license allowing the purchaser to build the plan as many times as desired, and a promotional license granting the right to produce the camera-ready art work for promotional purposes. Today, Design Basics is nationally recognized through numerous awards, not only for their designs, but also for achievements in business management, corporate growth, sales, and the development of effective marketing

products. This growth and success, in turn, has helped Design Basics, Inc. define their mission statement, "Bringing People Home." All the design products and services as well as each employee are a part of a culminating effort to help people attain their dream home.

CARMICHAEL AND DAME

It was 1986 when two small-volume builders, Patrick Carmichael and Robert Dame, merged their efforts and began designing and building homes for Houston's upper-end housing market. Carmichael's forte was in finance and business management; Dame's was in translating buyers' ideas into exquisite designs. The blend of their natural talents led them to their design/build firm, Carmichael and Dame. In 1994, with more than 300 designs accumulated, Carmichael and Dame made the decision to market designs nationwide by teaming up with Design Basics, Inc. one of Americas leading home plan design firms.

Carmichael and Dame plans are nothing meticulous, averaging 20-35 pages in length with specifications as detailed as the dimension of every piece of moulding. Unlike most plan services, each of the designs have been built by its own building division, ensuring the structural soundness and buildability of each plan as a result, Carmichael and Dame is able to provide builders and consumers with both technical and construction support throughout the building process. In addition, elegant watercolor renderings are available for each of their designs, as well as a Contract Development package - a complete materials specifications and quantities reference guide. Through itsr products and designs, Carmichael and Dame hope to rekindle the passion for excellence. "One of my dreams is that the craftsman aspect of design will return to the building industry in America as it was before the turn of the century," Dame says. "Our company has tried to do that by providing designs and products with a higher level of detail, craftsmanship, architectural significance and quality."

ALAN MASCORD DESIGN ASSOCIATES, INC.

Founded in 1983, Alan Mascord Design Associates, Inc. has developed an outstanding reputation in the industry for providing innovative, buildable stock plans. Mascord first began working with local builders, providing them with great plans for their projects. Soon it became apparent that these homes could be marketed nationwide;they began a direct mail program to reach builders in other areas. This success led to publishing opportunities and soon the company's plans were being featured in several national magazines.

Always interested in providing the best possible plans available, Mascord has wholeheartedly embraced the Computer Aided Design (CAD) technology. Starting in 1986, everything Alan Mascord Design Associates, Inc. has drawn has been on CAD. This has greatly improved the quality of its drawings and the efficiency of the drafting staff. Mascord, a professional member of the A.I.B.D. and the National Association of Home Builders, has been designing homes for 25 years. "In addition to projects all over the country, many of our homes have been built in Japan by the Mitsui Company, one of the biggest builders in Japan," says Mascord.

MICHAEL E. NELSON AND ASSOCIATES, INC.

At Michael E. Nelson and Associates, Inc. creativity, craftsmanship and technology are combined to form a unique offering in the home plan industry. By utilizing computer-aided drawing technology, Michael E. Nelson and his staff produce accurate and complete designs for individuals, designers and home builders throughout the United States, producing quality designs for over ten years. Michael E. Nelson & Associates' blend of creativity and technology has brought the firm recognition through several national publications and from the American Institute of Building Designers.

A constant quest for customer satisfaction has driven Nelson and Associates to produce a portfolio of plans that meet the needs of a diverse marketplace. The vast collection of plans range from traditional to contemporary, and can be modified to suit the special needs of clients. This collection of plans brings years of experience and insight together to form an invaluable resource to home builders and individuals alike.

VAUGHN A. LAUBAN DESIGNS

Vaughn A. Lauban Designs was established in 1976 incorporating Southern traditional and Creole farmhouse styles into its designs, Vaughn A. Lauban Designs has flourished. The company's home style developed a national market with its "Back to Basics" designs. With stock plans in demand in all 50 states and several foreign countries, Vaughn A. Lauban purchased a small office building, expanded, and remodeled it to reflect this Early American feeling. "We still concentrate on the farmhouse designs, although now with additional designers on staff, Midwestern and European designs are drafted to satisfy a demanding market,"

says Vaughn A. Lauban.

SELECT HOME DESIGNS

With nearly 50 years of experience delivering top-quality and affordable residential designs to

the North American housing market, Select Home Designs is proud to continue that tradition. Since the company's inception in 1948, more than 350,000 new homes throughout North America and overseas have been built from Select Home Design plans. The Select Home Design team, however, is never content to rest on its laurels, and is constantly striving to develop the best new plans for today's lifestyles. With an outstanding collection of proven plans, virtually every architectural style and influence is represented, many featuring the latest design innovations: lavish master bathrooms, dramatic foyers, unique staircase designs, and generous use of outdoor living spaces such as decks, porches and patios. One of the most important features of a Select Home Designs plan is the flexibility it offers- which is always an important factor to consider when building a new home.

FILLMORE DESIGN GROUP

Fillmore Design Group was formed in

1960 by Robert L. Fillmore, president and founder. Over the years, the firm has grown to 12 designers and draftspeople. Fillmore designs are often characterized by their European influences, massive brick gables and high flowing, graceful roof lines". We spend considerable time on detail, particularly brick detail, and we often place a fireplace with decorative brick patterns along the front facade for focus and interest. In fact, this attention to detail extends inside the home and pays off in terms of handsome, finely wrought moulding, cornices, and other interior detailing," says Fillmore. "Each plan is done in our office by one of our experienced designers under close supervision and is checked and rechecked for accuracy before leaving the office," explains Fillmore. "Each plan is carefully thought out, down to the smallest detail by our design group. We pay attention to such items as traffic flow, open rooms with tall ceiling heights and window openings, while at the same time think of

furniture placement and wall space. We try to allow plenty of storage areas, large kitchens with good work patterns, luxurious and exciting master baths and spacious master bedrooms." Fillmore Design Group belongs to the American Institute of Building Designers and the National Association of Home Builders. The company's work has been featured in various national publications.

How To Work With An Interior Designer

The preliminaries

People hire interior designers for a variety of reasons. Some people realize that they don't have the skill or imagination to handle the job. Others don't have the time. And still others want an image - "drop-dead" chic, slick contemporary, or "instant-heritage" traditional. They hire a designer known for a particular look who can help them achieve the image they want.

A good interior designer is an interpreter who translates your *tastes* and needs into an environment that is comfortable, functional, and pleasing to look at.

The specifics

Shortly after agreeing to work with you, the designer will probably draw up a contract.

Although there is no set system of fees in the interior design business, most designers charge clients in one of several ways, or in combination:

By the hour: Some designers charge by the hour when the job is small. Others charge by the hour regardless of the scope of the job.

Flat fee: Usually arrived at based on the extent of the work and the amount of time the designer gauges it will take to complete the job.

Percentage: Some designers charge a percentage of what the total job - concept, labor, and materials - will cost, usually 20 to 30 percent, as their design fee.

Mark-up: If not charged hourly, services will be included in the retail price.

It is the designer's responsibility to come up with a plan that fits your budget. If the estimates for the job come in higher than the original budget, it's up to the designer to rework the design so that it stays in line with the amount you originally intended to spend.

Your role

Realize that the interior designer is one the last custom professionals. The dressmaker, milliner, and bootmaker have all vanished. But the interior designer continues to produce custo one-of-a-kind design work. Custom work takes time.

You should also be aware that the inte designer is an intermediary. He or she relies o fleet of other professionals - painters, upholster and specialized craftsmen - to get the job done Foul-ups do occur. The sofa may get delayed a the upholsterer's. The painter may get backed in his work schedule. The custom-dyed fabric was supposed to be delicate peach could arrive bright orange. Be prepared for setbacks.

You can sit passively by and let the designer choose everything for you. But, if you get engaged in the process, it will be much mo exciting. Most designers welcome the client wl shows an active interest as the transformation takes place. Working with the designer to selec accent pieces, accessories, and antiques is the b way to become involved in the process, since it allows you to add your personality to the envir ment the professional is creating. And it's a sur way to be entirely satisfied with the final look c the room.

Carol J. Guess, ISID

Please, Help Us To Help You

In order to ensure that our Design America series best serves your needs, please assist us by filling out the questionnaire below. As a token of our appreciation, we'll send you a **FREE CATALOG** of **Project Plan Ideas**. (Please check the correct responses.)

1. Is this book your
   - ❏ 1st home plan book
   - ❏ 2nd home plan book
   - ❏ 3rd home plan book
   - ❏ _____ plan book

2. What prompted you to buy this Design America book?
   - ❏ Number of plans offered
   - ❏ Various plan styles
   - ❏ Customization
   - ❏ Looking for building ideas
   - ❏ Book category
   - ❏ Helpful articles

3. How long have you been searching for your dream home plan?
   - ❏ 0 - 6 months
   - ❏ 7 - 12 months
   - ❏ 12 - 24 months
   - ❏ More than two years

4. Would you like information on financing your dream home?
   - ❏ Yes
   - ❏ No

5. Are you looking for land to build on, if so, where?
   - ❏ Yes _____
   _____

6. When do you plan to begin construction of your new home?
   - ❏ 0 - 6 months
   - ❏ 6 - 12 months
   - ❏ Within 2 years
   - ❏ Not sure, gathering materials

7. How much do you plan to spend on materials on your new home (excluding land)?
   - ❏ Less than $100,000
   - ❏ $100,000 - $149,000
   - ❏ $150,000 - $199,000
   - ❏ More than $200,000

8. What style of home do you plan on building?
   - ❏ Traditional   ❏ Multi Family
   - ❏ Colonial   ❏ Country
   - ❏ Contemporary ❏ Vacation
   - ❏ Ranch   ❏ Victorian
   - ❏ Other _____

9. What additional information could we provide that would make it easier for you to build your dream home? (Please check all that apply)
   - ❏ Rear elevations
   - ❏ Interior elevations
   - ❏ Colored photographs of the homes
   - ❏ Approximate cost to build
   - ❏ More articles related to the home building process.
   - ❏ Other_____

10. Are you a . . . ?
   - ❏ Consumer   ❏ Building Trades
   - ❏ Professional Builder/Contractor

11. In what type of residence do you currently live?
   - ❏ Single family home   ❏ Townhouse
   - ❏ Condo / co-op   ❏ Apartment
   - ❏ Other

12. The population of the city, town you currently reside?
   - ❏ less than 20,000   ❏ 83,000-100,000
   - ❏ 21,000-41,000   ❏ 101,000- +
   - ❏ 42,000-82,000

13. What is your gross annual household income - before taxes?
   - ❏ Under $30,000
   - ❏ $31,000 - $60,000
   - ❏ $61,000 - $80,000
   - ❏ $81,000 - $100,000
   - ❏ $101,000 +

Mail or fax to: *NATIONAL PLAN SERVICE USA, INC., 222 JAMES ST., BENSENVILLE, IL 60106*

NAME _____

ADDRESS _____   *PLEASE FAX TO*   **1-800-344-4293**

CITY _____

STATE _____   ZIP _____   PHONE (_____) _____

Design America
Your Blueprints For Success

Our Blueprint Package contains nearly everything you need to get the job done properly and accurately, whether you're acting as your own general contractor or with help from an architect, designer, builder or subcontractors. Each Blueprint Package is the result of many hours of work by licensed architects or professional designers.

ACCURACY & QUALITY

Our staff of architects and professional designers have developed blueprints to ensure accuracy and quality.

VALUE

Purchase professional quality blueprints at a fraction of their development cost. With Design America, your dream home plan is attainable.

PROMPT SERVICE

Once you've chosen your dream home plan, fax your order to 1-800-344-4293 or call toll free at 1-800-533-4350. Upon receipt of your order, we will process it quickly!

SATISFACTION

With over 80 years of quality service to home plan buyers; past, present, and future, our experience and knowledge have made us a premier home plan company.

ORDER TOLL FREE
1-800-533-4350 or Fax 1-800-344-4293

After you've chosen your home plan package, simply mail or fax the accompanying order form on page 33 or call toll free on our Blueprint Hotline: 1-800-533-4350. We're ready to assist you in building your dream home.

- **HOUSE SECTIONS**
- **DETAILED FLOOR PLANS**
- **EXTERIOR ELEVATIONS**
- **INTERIOR ELEVATIONS**
- **FOUNDATION PLANS**
- **COVER SHEETS**
- **MATERIAL LIST**

Each set of blueprints is a collection of floor plans, exterior & interior elevations, details, cross-sections, diagrams and general notes showing precisely how your house is to be constructed.

Your Plans Will Show:

Cover Sheet

This artist's sketch of the exterior of the house, done in perspective, gives you an idea of how the house will look after it is built. This is only an artistic conception and may vary from actual working drawings.

Exterior Elevations

Drawn in 1/4-inch or 1/8-inch scale show the front, rear and sides of your house. General notes on exterior materials and finishes. A generic site plan may be incorporated in your blueprints.

Foundation Plan

Drawn to 1/4-inch scale, this sheet shows the complete foundation layout including support walls, excavated and unexcavated areas, if any, and foundation details. Specify slab construction, basement, or crawl when ordering.

Detailed Floor Plans

Completed in 1/4-inch scale, these plans show the layout of each floor of the house. All rooms and interior spaces are carefully dimensioned and keys are provided for cross-section details given later in the plans. The positions of all electrical outlets and switches are incorporated in this sheet.

House Sections

Large-scale cut-away views, normally drawn at 3/8-inch or 1/2-inch equals 1 foot, show sections or cut-away of the foundation, interior walls, exterior walls, floors, and roof areas. Additional cross-sections are given to show important changes in floor, ceiling or roof heights or the relationship of one level to another. Extremely valuable for construction, these sections show how the various parts of the house fit together.

Interior Elevations

These large-scale drawings show the design and placement of kitchen and bathroom cabinets, laundry areas, fireplaces, bookcases and other features. Little "extras," such as mantelpiece and wainscoting drawings, plus moulding sections, provide details that give your home that custom touch.

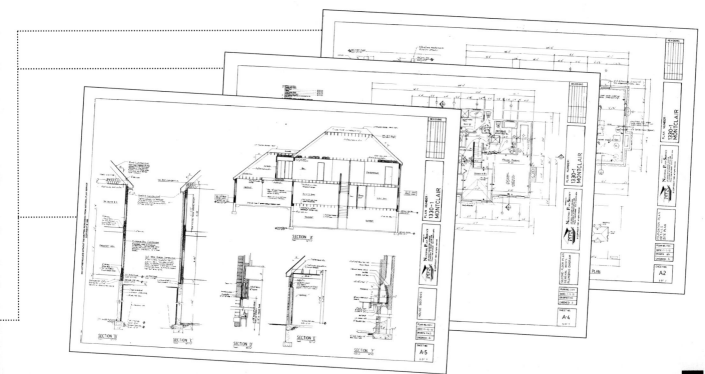

Design America Options and Services

Reversed

As Shown

Reversed Plans

Have you ever thought you've found the perfect home plan only the garage or porch is on the wrong side? The solution to this problem is in reversed, or "mirror image" plans. We can send one full set of "mirror image" plans (although the text will appear backwards) as a master guide for you and your builder.

Modifying Your Design America Home Plan

If you are considering making major changes to your design, we strongly recommend that you purchase our reproducible vellums and use the services of a professional designer, architect or ask our Design America staff. For this valuable service please call **1-800-533-4350 Architectural Dept.**

Our Reproducible Vellums and Mylars Make Modifications Easy

With a reproducible copy of our plans, a design professional can alter the drawings just the way you want. You can print as many copies of the modified plans as you need. And, since you have already started with our complete detailed plans, the cost of expensive professional services will be significantly less. Refer to the price schedule for vellums and mylars.

Don't Forget To Order Your Materials List

Our material list can help you save money. Available at a modest additional charge, the Materials List provides the quantity, dimensions, and specifications for the major materials needed to build your home. You will get faster, more accurate bids from your contractors and building suppliers. Materials Lists are available for most home plans, and can only be ordered with a set of plans. Due to differences in regional requirements and homeowner or builder preferences; electrical, plumbing and heating/ air conditioning equipment specifications are not designed specifically for each plan.

Financing Your New Home Program

Questions? Call our mortgage specialist at **1-800-533-4350**

Interior Design Services

Looking for the right image for your new home? We can help you with the right interior design image for your new home! Call our interior design expert at **1-800-533-4350**

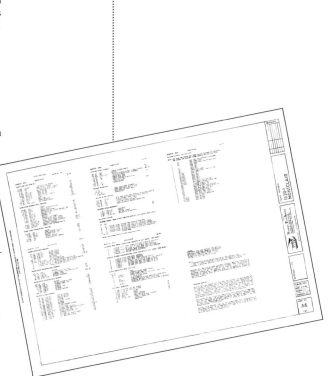

How Many Sets Of Plans Will You Need?

Single-Set Package

We offer this set so you can study the blueprints to plan your dream home in detail. Please NOTE that the Plans in this publication are copyrighted, therefore the plans cannot be reproduced. **Ignoring Copyright laws can be a costly mistake.**

The Standard 4-Set Construction Package

- First set is for yourself.
- Second set is for your builder.
- Third set is for your village or municipality.*
- Fourth set is for your bank.

The Contractor 7-Set Construction Package

- First set is for yourself.
- Second set is for your builder.
- Third set is for your village or municipality.*
- Fourth set is for your bank.
- Fifth set is for a plumbing contractor.
- Sixth set is for a heating contractor.
- Seventh set is for additional bids.

Generic Details for the Home Builder

Because local codes and requirements vary greatly, we recommend that you obtain drawings and bids from licensed contractors to complete your mechanical plans. However, if you want to know more about techniques— and deal more confidently with subcontractors—we offer these remarkably useful detail sheets. Each is an excellent tool that will enhance your understanding of these technical subjects.

Residential Construction Details

Eight sheets feature the essentials of stick-built residential home construction. Detailed foundation options - poured concrete basement, concrete block, or monolithic concrete slab. Shows all aspects of floor, wall, and roof framing. Provides details for roof dormer, eaves, and skylights. Conforms to requirements of Uniform Building code or BOCA code.

$14.95 each

Residential Plumbing Details

Nine sheets packed with information on pipe connection methods, fittings, and sizes. Shows sump pump and water softener hookups, and septic system construction. Conforms to requirements of National Plumbing Code. Color coded with a glossary of terms.   **$14.95** each

Residential Electrical Details

Nine sheets that depict all aspects of residential wiring, from simple switch wiring to the complexities of three-phase and service entrance connection. Explains service load calculations and distribution panel wiring. Shows you how to create a floor plan wiring diagram. Conforms to requirements of National Electrical Code. Color coded with a glossary of terms.

$14.95 each

Detail Plan Prices

Purchase any two (2) sets for only $22.96 or all three (3) for $29.97. See the Order Form on page 33.

Important Shipping Information

Your order is processed immediately. Allow 10 working days from our receipt of your order for normal UPS delivery. Save time with your credit card and our "800" number. UPS must have a street address or Rural Route Box number—never a post office box. Use a work address if no one is home during the day. Please call for international shipping information.

AN IMPORTANT NOTE:

1) All plans are drawn to conform to one or more of the building industry's major national building standards at the time and place they were drawn. However, due to the variety of local building regulations, your plan may need to be modified to comply with local requirements—snow loads, energy loads, seismic zones, etc. We strongly recommend that you consult with your local building officials or local architect for required information on submission of permit documents.
2) Detail plans are generic and do not conform specifically to the house plan that you purchase.

*Multiple sets of documents (blueprints) may be required by your local village or municipality building depts.

1. **Choose your Design America Plan**

2. **Would you like to customize your blueprints to your family's needs and lifestyle?**

   If YES: Talk to one of our blueprints experts at 1-800-533-4350 or in Illinois 630-238-0555

   If NO: Order the design number indicated at the top of the page, determine number of sets needed and specify if you are ordering a plan with foundation options; basement, crawl space, slab, pier.

3. **Upon having made your decision as to the design you wish to purchase, we recommend you order them through the Lumber yard, Home Center, or Hardware dealer who provided you with this book. Your local Lumber yard, Home Center, or Hardware dealer can give you valuable information and suggestions on you new dream home. Or mail, phone or fax us your blueprint order or customization request and we will process your order quickly. For accurate processing of your order please enclose check, money order, cashiers check or Master card/Visa information with the plan design number and order form (Page 33) To:**

NPS Design America, Inc.
Slot A-1
P.O. Box 66973 **DA 1000**
Chicago, Illinois 60666-0973
Ph. 1-800-533-4350 • 630-238-0555
Fax 1-800-344-4293 • 630-238-8885

Blueprint Prices

The cost of having an architect design a new custom home typically runs from 4 to 10 percent of the total construction cost, or from $4,000 to $10,000 for a $100,000 home. A single set of blueprints for the plans in this book ranges from $195 to $720, depending on the size of the house. Working with existing drawings may save you enough money on design fees to enable you to build a deck, upgrade your materials, or design a luxurious kitchen. Please note : garages, porches, decks, and unfinished basements are not included with the total living area, unless noted.

What will it cost to Build?

As noted in one of the articles, it is best to find out how much you can qualify for prior to building. Building cost vary widely from region to region, depending on a number of factors, including local material availability and labor costs, and the finished materials selected.

Foundation Options & Exterior Construction

Depending on your site conditions and region, your home will be built with a slab, pier, pole, crawlspace, or basement foundation. Exterior walls will be framed with either 2 by 4's or 2 by 6's, determined by structural and insulation standards in your area. Consult with your local building official in your area. Most contractors can easily adapt a home to meet the foundation and/or wall requirements for your area.

Service & Blueprint Delivery

Blueprint representatives are available to answer questions and assist you in placing your order. Plans are delivered via U.S. Mail or UPS.

Returns & Exchanges

Blueprints are specially printed and shipped to you in response to your specific order, consequently, requests for refunds cannot be honored.

Local Codes & Regulations

Because of climactic, geographic, and governmental policies set by your municipality, building codes and regulations vary from one area to another. These plans are authorized for your use only on the expressed consent that you oblige and agree to comply with all local building codes, ordinances, regulations, and requirements, including permits and inspections at time of construction.

Architectural & Engineering Seals

With increased concern about energy cost and safety, many cities and states require that an architect or engineer review and "seal" a blueprint prior to construction. To find whether this is a requirement in your area, contact your local building department.

License Agreement, Copy Restrictions & Copyright

When you purchase your blueprints, you are granted the right to use these documents to construct a single unit. All the plans in this publication are protected under the Federal Copyright Act, Title XVII of the United States Code and Chapter 37 of the Code of Federal Regulations.   Each designer retains title and ownership of the original documents. The blueprints licensed to you cannot be used by or resold to any other person, copied, or reproduced by any means. The copying restrictions do not apply to reproducible blueprints. When you purchase a reproducible set of mylars or vellums, you may modify and reproduce it for your own use.

AN IMPORTANT NOTE:

1) All plans are drawn to conform to one or more of the building industry's major national building standards at the time and place they were drawn. However, due to the variety of local building regulations, your plan may need to be modified to comply with local requirements—snow loads, energy loads, seismic zones, etc. We strongly recommend that you consult with your local building officials or local architect for required information on submission of permit documents.
2) Detail plans are generic and do not conform specifically to the house plan that you purchase.

*Multiple sets of documents (blueprints) may be required by your local village or municipality building depts.

P R I C E   C O D E*

	A	B	C	D	E	F
BLUEPRINTS (Material List subject to availability)						
One Set of Blueprints	$195.00	$230.00	$275.00	$320.00	$520.00	$720.00
Four Sets of Blueprints	$265.00	$310.00	$355.00	$400.00	$1,020.00	$1,220.00
Seven Sets of Blueprints	$320.00	$360.00	$405.00	$450.00	$1,420.00	$1,620.00
Reproducible Vellum (1 Set)	$480.00	$540.00	$600.00	$675.00	$1,645.00	$1,845.00
Reproducible Mylar (1Set)	$500.00	$560.00	$620.00	$695.00	$1,665.00	$1,865.00
Additional regular sets	$40.00	$40.00	$40.00	$40.00	$180.00	$180.00
Mirror reverse	$40.00	$40.00	$40.00	$40.00	$180.00	$180.00
SHIPPING AND HANDLING 1–7 sets						
Regular U.S.(6-10 days)	$10.00	$13.00	$16.00	$19.00	$22.00	$25.00
Express (2-3 days)	$25.00	$28.00	$31.00	$34.00	$37.00	$40.00
Overnight*	$30.00	$33.00	$36.00	$39.00	$42.00	$45.00
Other**	Call	Call	Call	Call	Call	Call
*Not available on certain plans **For delivery outside U.S.						
MATERIAL LIST *Material list subject to availability						
1-3 copies	$40.00	$40.00	$40.00	$40.00	CALL	CALL
4-7 copies	$45.00	$45.00	$45.00	$45.00	CALL	CALL
PREVIEW PLANS (11" X 17" format)						
1 ea. B/W format*	$15.00	$15.00	$15.00	$15.00	CALL	CALL
1 ea. Colored format* *Subject to availability	$40.00	$40.00	$40.00	$40.00	CALL	CALL
DESIGN SHEETS (8.5" X 11" format)						
1 ea. B/W sell sheets*	$25.00	$25.00	$25.00	$25.00	—	—
100 qty. ea. B/W sell sheets*	$38.00	$38.00	$38.00	$38.00	—	—
200 qty. ea. B/W sell sheets*	$58.00	$58.00	$58.00	$58.00	—	—
ARCHITECTURAL RENDERING OF HOME						
B/W 8"X10" PMT Format*	$89.00	$89.00	$89.00	$89.00	CALL	CALL
Colored 8"X10" PMT format*	$115.00	$115.00	$115.00	$115.00	CALL	CALL

*Subject to availability

Step 1.

BLUEPRINTS ORDER FORM

PURCHASED BOOK FROM: _____ TOWN: _____

DATE BOOK WAS PURCHASED: _____

NAME: _____

ADDRESS: _____

CITY: _____ STATE: _____ ZIP: _____

PHONE #: (___) _____

Enclosed is: ☐Check ☐Money Order
Bill: ☐Visa ☐Master Card

Checks Payable to: NPS Design America, Inc.

CARD NUMBER: _____

EXPIRATION DATE MONTH/YEAR_____/_____

SIGNATURE _____

Step 2.

Plan Number _____ Price Code_____

Foundation Type:_____
(Many plans offer different options; others are designed to one type of condition).

Number of Sets: ____One Set ____Four Sets ____Seven Sets ____Vellum ____Mylar

Additional Sets: _____ Qty. ($40.00 Price Code A-D; Price Code E-F Call) Prices good for 60 days

Mirror Reverse:_____ ($40.00)

Material List: _____(See List)

Preview Plan Number: _____ (See List)

Design Sheets: ____1ea. ____100 qty. ____200 qty. of Plan Number:_____
(Check appropriate space)

Architectural Rendering: _____B/W _____Colored (See List) Plan Number:_____

Send Your Order To: NPS Design America, Inc.
Slot A-1 P.O. Box 66973 Dept. DA1000, Chicago, IL, 60666-0973

Order Toll Free 1-800-533-4350 Or 24-Hour Fax Ordering 1-800-344-4293

Step 3.

Detail Plans

_____**H801C Construction**
@ $14.95 each
_____**H802E Electrical**
@ $14.95 each
_____**H803P Plumbing**
@ $14.95 each
Any two (2) - $22.96
Any three (3) - $29.97

Write in dollar figure

$_____ Detail plans

$_____ Blueprints

$_____ Material List

$_____ Preview Plans

$_____ Design Sheets

$_____ Arch Rendering

$_____ Shipping & Handling

$_____ Sub Total

$_____ Sales Tax (IL 6.75%)

$_____ **Total**

*Prices may change without notice

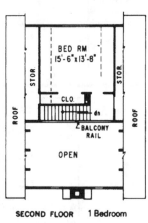

BED RM
15'-6" x 13'-8"

STOR.   STOR.

ROOF   CLO.   ROOF

dn

BALCONY RAIL

OPEN

SECOND FLOOR   1 Bedroom

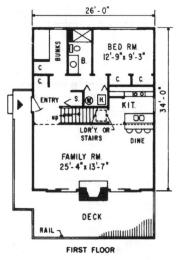

26'-0"

BUNKS   BED RM.
12'-9" x 9'-3"

C   B.
C
C   C   C

ENTRY   S.   K   H   KIT.

up   34'-0"

LDR'Y. OR STAIRS   DINE

FAMILY RM.
25'-4" x 13'-7"

DECK

RAIL

FIRST FLOOR

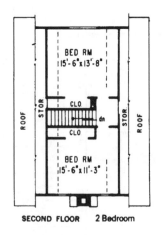

BED RM
15'-6" x 13'-8"

STOR.   CLO.   STOR.

ROOF   dn   ROOF
CLO.

BED RM
15'-6" x 11'-3"

SECOND FLOOR   2 Bedroom

Cross Section
1 BED RM.

Plan with 3 Bedroom
First Floor   884 sq. ft.
Second Floor   550 sq. ft.
Total Living Area   1,434 sq. ft.

Plan with 2 Bedroom
First Floor   884 sq. ft.
Second Floor   327 sq. ft.
Total Living Area   1,211 sq. ft.

PRICE CODE: A

PLAN SH91-1322

35

ldr

FUTURE RECREATION ROOM

FUTURE DEVELOPMENT

LINE OF FLOOR OVER

W
D

F H

STORAGE

LINE OF BAY WINDOW OVER

LOWER LEVEL

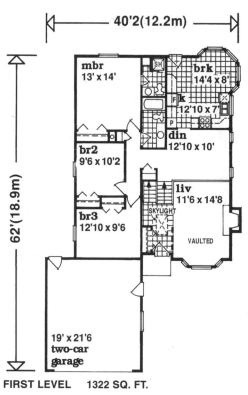

40'2(12.2m)

62'(18.9m)

mbr 13' x 14'

brk 14'4 x 8'

SH

k 12'10 x 7'

din 12'10 x 10'

br2 9'6 x 10'2

liv 11'6 x 14'8

br3 12'10 x 9'6

SKYLIGHT

VAULTED

19' x 21'6 **two-car garage**

P

FIRST LEVEL   1322 SQ. FT.

Features

- Handsome starter or retirement home with added features.
- Vaulted living room, with fireplace and bay window, plan shares one level with the skylit foyer.
- Railed dining room overlooks the living room.

- Efficient kitchen has a breakfast carousel and access to rear yard.
- Master bedroom has private ensuite with plan shower.

Total Living Area   1,322 sq. ft.

PRICE CODE: B

CUSTOMIZE IT!

ORDER TOLL FREE 1▪800▪533▪4350   **24-HOUR FAX ORDERING** 1▪800▪344▪4293

PLAN SH90-1381

36

**BASEMENT STAIR
LOCATION**

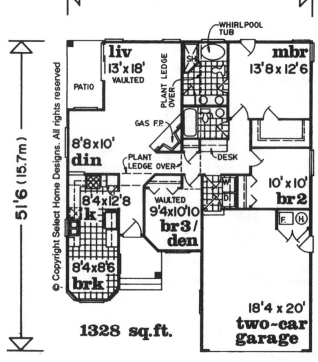

42' (12.8m)

51'6 (15.7m)

WHIRLPOOL TUB

liv 13'x18' VAULTED

PLANT LEDGE OVER

mbr 13'8 x 12'6

PATIO

SH

GAS F.P.

PLANT LEDGE OVER

DESK

8'8x10' **din**

PLANT LEDGE OVER

10' x 10' **br2**

k 8'4x12'8

VAULTED 9'4x10'10 **br3/ den**

W D

F. H.

8'4x8'6 **brk**

1328 sq.ft.

18'4 x 20' **two~car garage**

Features

- Designed to capture the view to the rear of the lot.
- Home may be finished in California stucco or horizontal siding.
- Kitchen, with abundant counter space and passthrough to the dining room, adjoins the breakfast bay.
- Plant ledge over the entry adorns the dining room.

- Living room features corner positioned fireplace and sliding glass door to the garden patio.
- Clerestory window brightens third bedroom or den.
- Master bedroom boasts a walk-in closet, French door to the garden and ensuite with twin vanity and spa.

Total Living Area   1,328 sq. ft.

PRICE CODE: B

CUSTOMIZE IT!

ORDER TOLL FREE   **1■800■533■4350**   24-HOUR FAX ORDERING   **1■800■344■4293**

PLAN NP1349

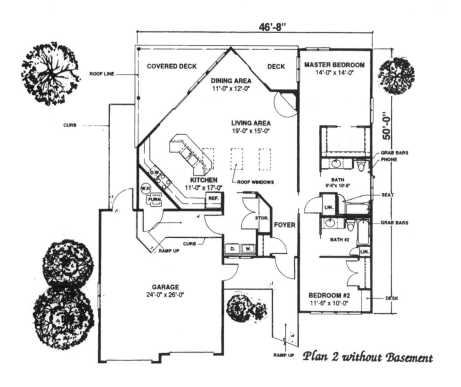

46'-8"

COVERED DECK — DECK — MASTER BEDROOM
14'-0" x 14'-0"

ROOF LINE

DINING AREA
11'-0" x 12'-0"

CURB

LIVING AREA
19'-0" x 15'-0"

50'-0"

D.W.

KITCHEN
11'-0" x 17'-0"

GRAB BARS
PHONE

ROOF WINDOWS

W.H.

FURN.

BATH
9'-6" x 10'-9"

REF.

SEAT

LIN.

STOR.

FOYER

GRAB BARS

CURB

D. W.

BATH #2

RAMP UP

LIN.

GARAGE
24'-0" x 26'-0"

BEDROOM #2
11'-6" x 10'-0"

DESK

RAMP UP

Plan 2 without Basement

Paramount Estate

Features

- Striking contemporary design offers complete handicap accessibility.
- Deep, two-car garage offers ramp access into utility room.
- Main entryway is via ramped front porch into foyer.
- Foyer leads to a combined kitchen/ dining/living area illuminated by three large roof windows.
- Rear of home features two, separate covered decks for ultimate in relaxation and outdoor leisure.
- Both bathrooms, located in right wing, feature grab bars and sliding door access.

Total Living Area **1,340 sq. ft.**

PRICE CODE: B

CUSTOMIZE IT!

ORDER TOLL FREE 1▪800▪533▪4350   24-HOUR FAX ORDERING 1▪800▪344▪4293

PLAN MN1353

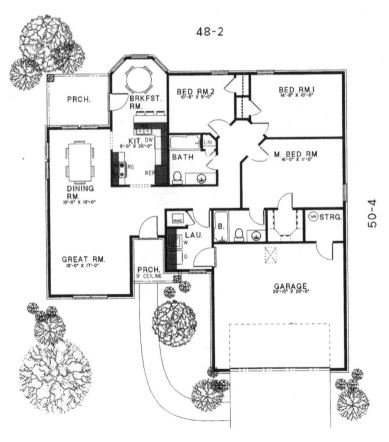

48-2

PRCH.

BRKFST. RM.

BED RM.2
10'-6" X 9'-0"

BED RM.1
14'-8" X 10'-0"

KIT. DW
9'-0" X 20'-0"

LIN

BATH

M. BED RM.
16'-0" X 11'-0"

DINING RM.
10'-0" X 10'-0"

RG

REF

HVAC

STRG.
WH

GREAT RM.
13'-0" X 17'-0"

LAU.
W
D

B.

PRCH.
9' CEILING

GARAGE
20'-10" X 20'-0"

50-4

Total Living Area   1,353 sq. f

PLAN NP WOODRIDGE

39

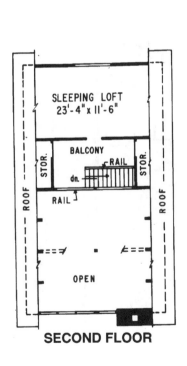

SECOND FLOOR

- SLEEPING LOFT 23'-4" x 11'-6"
- BALCONY
- RAIL
- dn.
- RAIL
- STOR.
- STOR.
- ROOF
- ROOF
- OPEN

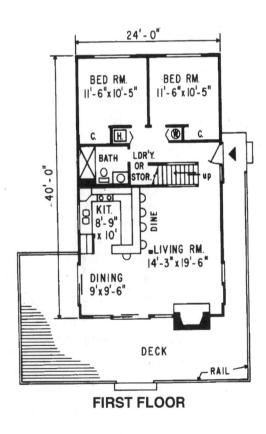

FIRST FLOOR

- 24'-0"
- 40'-0"
- BED RM. 11'-6" x 10'-5"
- BED RM. 11'-6" x 10'-5"
- C.
- H.
- W.
- C.
- BATH
- LDR'Y. OR STOR.
- up
- KIT. 8'-9" x 10'
- DINE
- LIVING RM. 14'-3" x 19'-6"
- DINING 9' x 9'-6"
- DECK
- RAIL

First Floor   960 sq. ft.
Second Floor   394 sq. ft.
Total Living Area   1,354 sq. ft.

PRICE CODE: B

PLAN FD7018

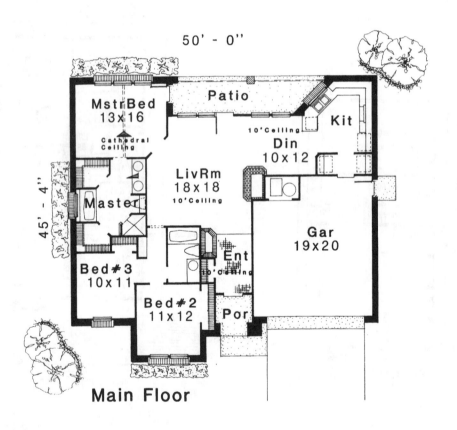

Main Floor

50' - 0''

45' - 4''

MstrBed 13x16
Cathedral Ceiling

Patio

Kit

10'Ceiling

Din 10x12

LivRm 18x18
10'Ceiling

Master

Gar 19x20

Bed#3 10x11

Ent
10'Ceiling

Bed#2 11x12

Por

Total Living Area   1,417 sq. ft.

40

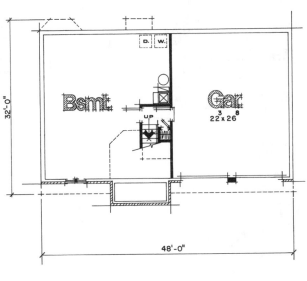

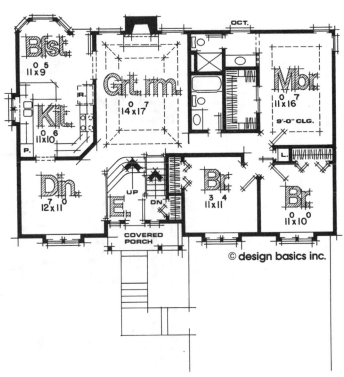

41

© design basics inc.

Features

- Optional elevation included with this plan at no additional cost.
- Formal dining room open to large entry with coat closet and wide stairs.
- Great room with vaulted ceiling and fireplace as focal point.
- Double L-shaped kitchen includes boxed win dow at sink, pantry, space saver microwave and buffet counter.
- Convenient split-entry ranch design.
- Core hallway opens to large master bedroom with walk-in closet and private bath.
- Secondary bedrooms feature boxed windows and share centrally located hall bath.

Total Living Area   1,429 sq. ft.

PRICE CODE: C

CUSTOMIZE IT!

ORDER TOLL FREE   1■800■533■4350   24-HOUR FAX ORDERING   1■800■344■4293

42

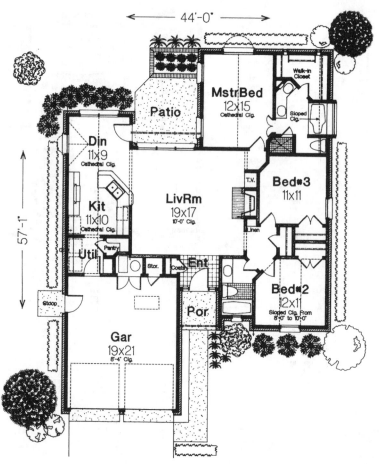

Total Living Area   1,431 sq. ft.

PRICE CODE: B

PLAN SH1688-1495

43

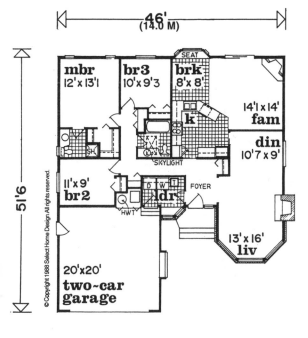

46'
(14.0 M)

mbr
12' x 13'1

br3
10' x 9'3

SEAT
brk
8' x 8'

k

14'1 x 14'
fam

din
10'7 x 9'

SKYLIGHT

11' x 9'
br2

ldr
FOYER

HWT

13' x 16'
liv

20' x 20'
two~car garage

51'6

1496 sq. ft.

12' x 9'
br2

W D
ldr

55'6 (16.9m)

20' x 20'
two~car garage

Basement stair location

Features

- Living room rests in a windowed-bay.
- Open plan kitchen has ample counter space.
- Cozy window seat tucked in the breakfast bay.
- Fireplace warms the family room.
- Master bedroom has a walk-in wardrobe and three-piece ensuite with shower.
- Main bathroom has a skylight.
- Plan includes a basement and crawlspace foundation.

Total Living Area   **1,496 sq. ft.**

PRICE CODE: B

44

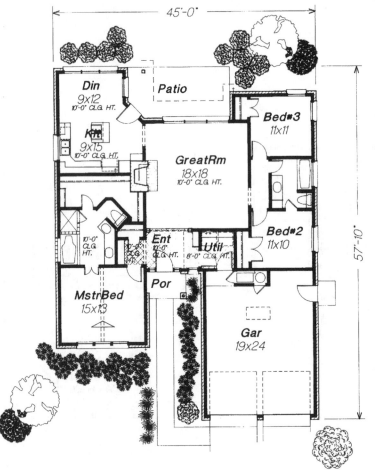

45'-0"

57'-10"

Din
9x12
10'-0" CLG. HT.

Patio

Kit
9x15
10'-0" CLG. HT.

GreatRm
18x18
10'-0" CLG. HT.

Bed#3
11x11

10'-0"
CLG.
HT.

Ent
10'-0"
CLG. HT.

Util
8'-0" CLG. HT.

Bed#2
11x10

MstrBed
15x13

Por

Gar
19x24

Total Living Area   1,505 sq. ft.

PLAN NP1185

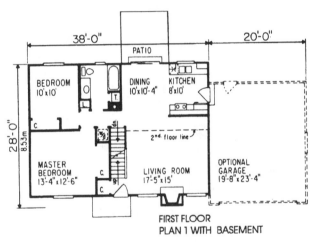

FIRST FLOOR
PLAN 1 WITH BASEMENT

45

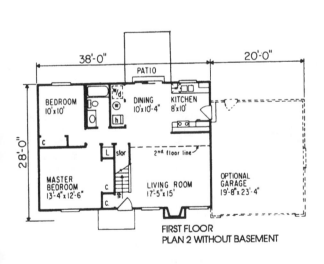

FIRST FLOOR
PLAN 2 WITHOUT BASEMENT

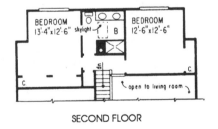

SECOND FLOOR

Quantico

Features

- Compact and stylish, this home is perfect for those with a limited budget.
- The two-car garage is optional and can be added later.
- Front door opens to a spacious living room with cathedral ceiling.

- Efficient kitchen with access outside or to optional garage.
- Second floor includes two bedrooms with full bath and skylight.

First Floor	988 sq. ft.
Second Floor	520 sq. ft.
Total Living Area	1,508 sq. ft.

PRICE CODE: B

CUSTOMIZE IT!

ORDER TOLL FREE 1■800■533■4350   24-HOUR FAX ORDERING   1■800■344■4293

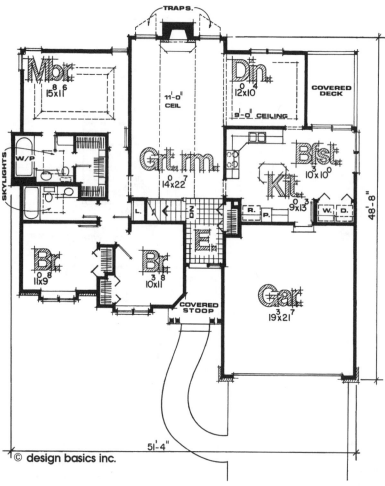

46

Features

- Dramatic high entry framed by columns and windows.
- Expansive great room features sloped ceilings to 11 feet and impressive fireplace surrounded by windows.
- Complete island kitchen includes lazy Susan, pantry and desk plus adjacent laundry area.
- Bright breakfast eating area.
- Formal ceiling in dining room.
- Vaulted ceiling in master bedroom with corner windows.
- Master bath features skylight and walk-in closet.
- Pleasant window sills in front bedroom.

© design basics inc.

Total Living Area   **1,511 sq. ft.**

PRICE CODE: C

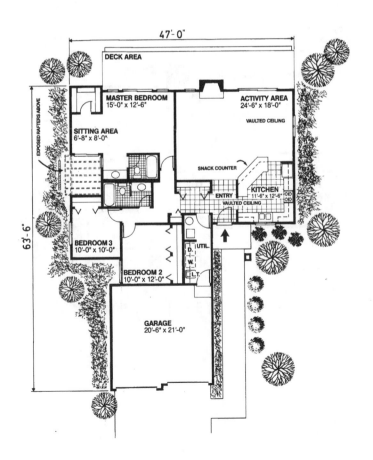

Features

- Multiple gabled roofs with dramatic overhangs add to the exterior charm of this three bedroom contemporary home.
- The interior is cozy, with plenty of features for folks who love outdoor living indoors.
- There's a private deck outside the master bedroom sitting area.
- Sloped ceilings add a sense of the great outdoors to the large activity area.
- The activity room also enjoys its own fireplace and snack bar and shares access to the backyard with the master bedroom.

Total Living Area   1,533 sq. ft.

PRICE CODE: B

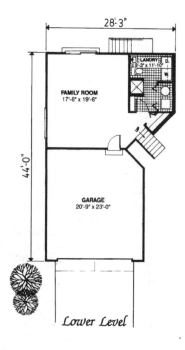

Lower Level

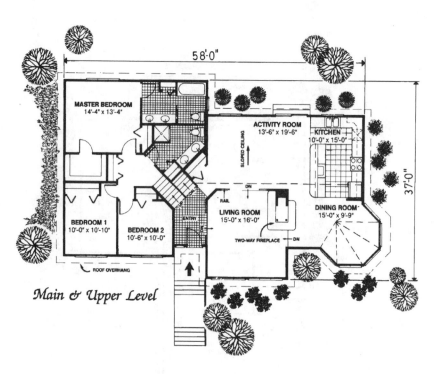

Main & Upper Level

Casa Rustique

Features

- This rustic, split-level home includes many outstanding features, such as wide roof overhangs and vertical windows.
- Master bedroom with compartmented bath and large walk-in closet.
- Two additional bedrooms share a deluxe bath.

- Sunken living room features two-way fireplace and entry to dining room with beautiful, huge circular windows.
- Sloped, cathedral-ceiling in the activity room.
- Entry down to lower level, where the large family room and laundry room is located.

Main Level	1,645 sq. ft.
Lower Level	520 sq. ft.
Total Living Area	2,165 sq. ft.

PRICE CODE: B

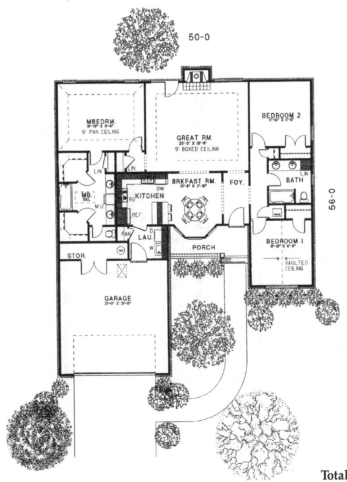

50-0

49

M.BEDRM.
16'-10" X 11'-6"
9' PAN CEILING

GREAT RM.
20'-0" X 15'-6"
9' BOXED CEILING

BEDROOM 2
11'-10" X 11'-0"

LIN

LIN

LIN

BATH

M.B.
5'KL.

KITCHEN

BRKFAST RM.
10'-8" X 11'-10"

FOY.

DW

RG

REF.

M.U.

D

PAN

LAU.

HVAC

STOR.

W

PORCH

BEDROOM 1
11'-10" X 11'-0"

VAULTED
CEILING

56-0

GARAGE
21'-0" X 21'-0"

Total Living Area   1,538 sq. ft.

CUSTOMIZE IT!

ORDER TOLL FREE   1 ▪ 800 ▪ 533 ▪ 4350   **24-HOUR FAX ORDERING**   1 ▪ 800 ▪ 344 ▪ 4293

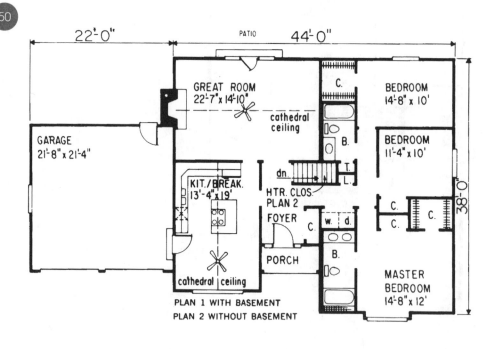

22'-0"   PATIO   **44'-0"**

GREAT ROOM
22'-7" x 14'-10"

cathedral ceiling

C.

BEDROOM
14'-8" x 10'

B.

GARAGE
21'-8" x 21'-4"

BEDROOM
11'-4" x 10'

T.
L.

dn.

KIT./BREAK.
13'-4" x 19'

HTR. CLOS.
PLAN 2

FOYER

C.

w.   d.

C.   C.

38'-0"

PORCH

B.

cathedral ceiling

MASTER
BEDROOM
14'-8" x 12'

PLAN 1 WITH BASEMENT
PLAN 2 WITHOUT BASEMENT

Lighted Charm

Features

- Porch entrance into foyer leads to an impressive dining area with full window with half-circle window above.
- Kitchen/breakfast room features a center island and cathedral ceiling.
- Great room with cathedral ceiling and exposed beams accessible from foyer.
- Master bedroom includes full bath and walk-in closet.
- Two additional bedrooms share a full bath.

Total Living Area   **1,540 sq. ft.**

PRICE CODE: B

CUSTOMIZE IT!

ORDER TOLL FREE   1 ■ 800 ■ 533 ■ 4350   **24-HOUR FAX ORDERING**   1 ■ 800 ■ 344 ■ 4293

Plans include all exteriors shown

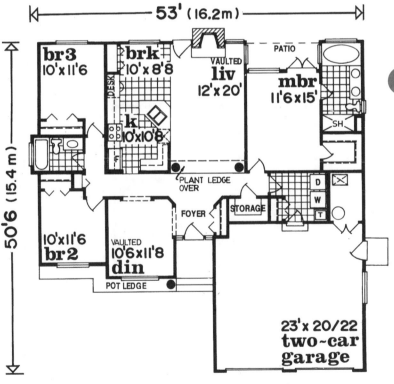

51

53' (16.2m)

50'6 (15.4 m)

br3 10'x 11'6

brk 10'x 8'8

DESK

VAULTED liv 12'x 20'

PATIO

mbr 11'6 x 15'

SH

k 10'x10'8

F

PLANT LEDGE OVER

br2 10'x 11'6

VAULTED 10'6 x 11'8 din

FOYER

STORAGE

D
W
T

POT LEDGE

23'x 20/22 two~car garage

Features

- Affordable ranch design offers a choice of exteriors – contemporary California stucco or horizontal siding with brick detailing.
- Tall, arched window wall accentuates the dining room's vaulted ceiling.
- Decorative columns topped with a plant ledge introduce the vaulted living room.
- Kitchen with angled sink, built-in desk and

pantry is open to the breakfast room.
- Master bedroom boasts French door access to the patio, walk-in closet and ensuite with twin vanity, plan shower and whirlpool spa.
- Two additional bedrooms plan share a main bathroom with soaking tub.

Total Living Area   1,550 sq. ft.

PRICE CODE: B

CUSTOMIZE IT!

ORDER TOLL FREE   1∎800∎533∎4350   24-HOUR FAX ORDERING   1∎800∎344∎4293

PLAN JA5499

 52

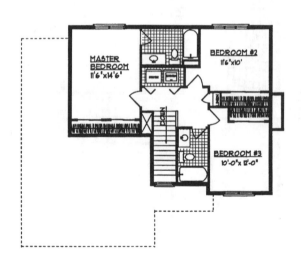

SECOND FLOOR PLAN

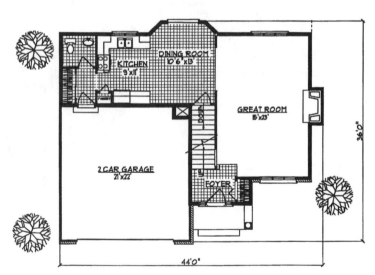

MAIN FLOOR PLAN

First Floor	811 sq. ft.
Second Floor	741 sq. ft.
Total Living Area	1,552 sq. ft.

PRICE CODE: B

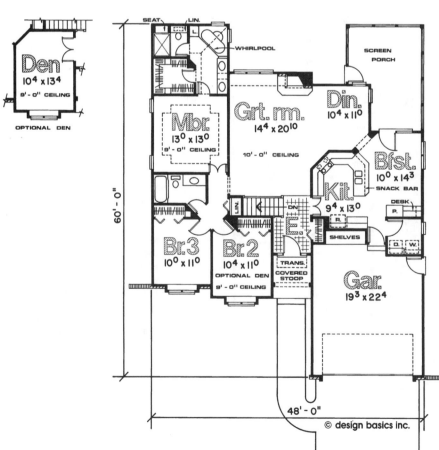

53

Features

- Brick wing walls provide visually expansive front elevation.
- From entry, traffic flows into bright great room with impressive 2-sided fireplace.
- Dining room opens to great room, offering view of fireplace.
- French doors off entry open into kitchen.
- Kitchen features large pantry, planning desk and snack bar.
- Dinette accesses large, comfortable screen porch.
- Laundry room is strategically located off kitchen and provides for direct access from garage.
- Built-in shelves in garage.
- French doors access master suite with formal ceiling and pampering bath.

Total Living Area   **1,580 sq. ft.**

PRICE CODE: C

CUSTOMIZE IT!

ORDER TOLL FREE   1▪800▪533▪4350   24-HOUR FAX ORDERING   1▪800▪344▪4293

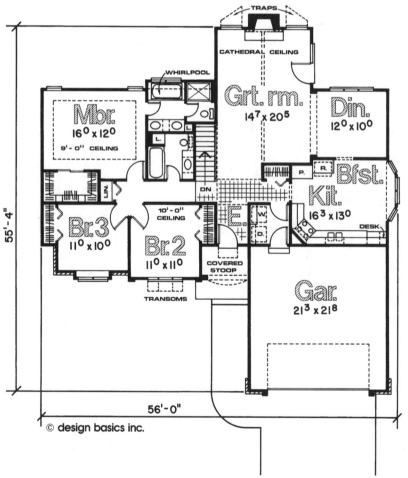

Features

- Crisp lines with subtle detailing enhance front elevation of this elegant ranch.
- Striking 10-foot-high entry has plant shelf integrated above closet.
- Cathedral ceiling and fireplace flanked by trapezoid windows highlight great room.
- Expansive great room, dining room, sunny kitchen/breakfast area encourage leisure and entertaining pursuits.
- Luxurious master suite benefits from ceiling detail and spacious walk-in closet with mirrored doors.
- Compartmented master bath features window to flood whirlpool and vanity/makeup area with natural light.

Total Living Area   1,583 sq. ft.

PRICE CODE: C

55

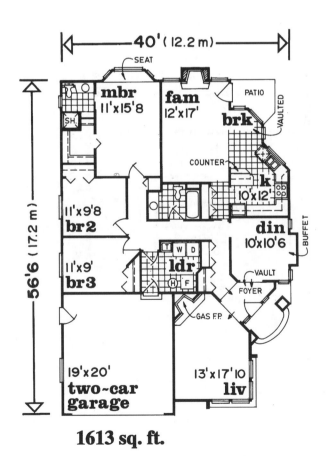

40' (12.2 m)

SEAT

mbr
11'x15'8

fam
12'x17'

PATIO

brk

VAULTED

SH.

COUNTER

56'6 (17.2 m)

11'x9'8
br2

k
10'x12'

din
10'x10'6

BUFFET

11'x9'
br3

T W D
ldr
H F

VAULT

FOYER

GAS F.P.

19'x20'
**two-car
garage**

13'x17'10
liv

1613 sq. ft.

Features

- Tall arched entry introduces a three bedroom design well suited for a corner lot.
- Raised foyer spills into the sunken livingroom with corner positioned fireplace.
- Archway leads from the foyer to the dining room.
- Island kitchen, with abundant counter space and pantry, serves a carrousel breakfast bay.
- Large family room is open to the kitchen and breakfast room.
- Master bedroom offers a window seat, walk-in closet and ensuite with shower.
- Two additional bedrooms share a main bathroom with soaking tub.

Total Living Area   1,613 sq. ft.

PRICE CODE: B

PLAN FD7099

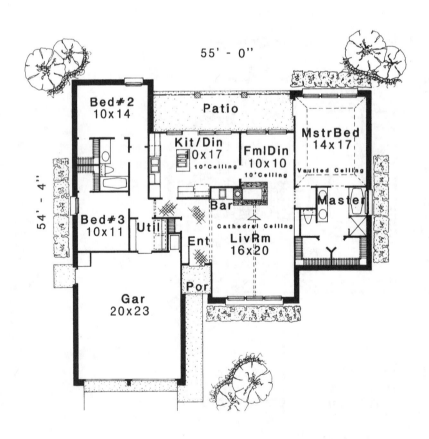

55' - 0''

54' - 4''

Bed #2
10x14

Patio

Kit/Din
10x17
10'Ceiling

FmlDin
10x10
10'Ceiling

MstrBed
14x17

Vaulted Ceiling

Bar

Master

Bed #3
10x11

Util

Ent

Cathedral Ceiling

LivRm
16x20

Gar
20x23

Por

Total Living Area   1,624 sq. ft.

PRICE CODE: B

PLAN JA5169

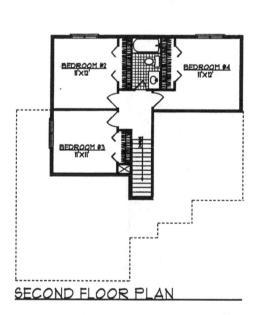

BEDROOM #2
11'x12'

BEDROOM #4
11'x12'

BEDROOM #3
11'x11'

SECOND FLOOR PLAN

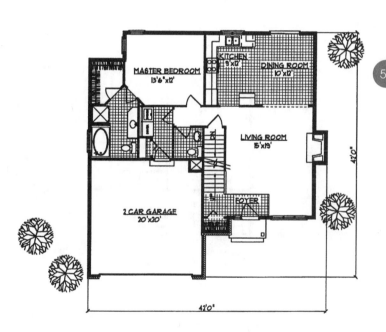

KITCHEN
9'x12'

MASTER BEDROOM
13'6"x12'

DINING ROOM
10'x12'

LIVING ROOM
15'x19'

2 CAR GARAGE
20'x20'

FOYER

42'0"

42'0"

57

MAIN FLOOR PLAN

First Floor	1,011 sq. ft.
Second Floor	621 sq. ft.
Total Living Area	1,632 sq. ft.

PRICE CODE: B

CUSTOMIZE IT!

ORDER TOLL FREE 1▪800▪533▪4350   24-HOUR FAX ORDERING   1▪800▪344▪4293

PLAN VL1646

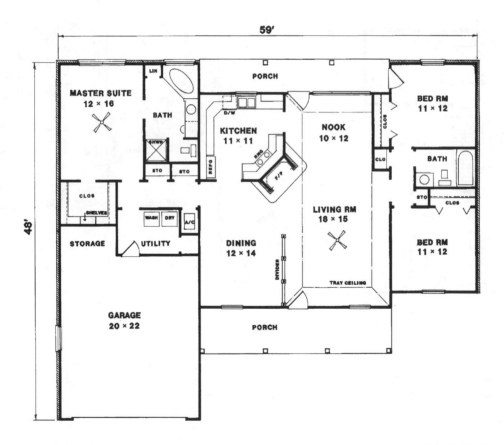

59'

48'

MASTER SUITE
12 × 16

LIN

BATH

SHWR

STO   STO

CLOS

SHELVES

STORAGE

WASH DRY A/C

UTILITY

D/W

KITCHEN
11 × 11

REFG

RNG

F/P

PORCH

NOOK
10 × 12

CLOS

CLO

BED RM
11 × 12

BATH

STO   CLOS

LIVING RM
18 × 15

BED RM
11 × 12

DINING
12 × 14

DIVIDER

TRAY CEILING

GARAGE
20 × 22

PORCH

Total Living Area   1,646 sq.

PRICE CODE: B

PLAN SH1189-1650

59

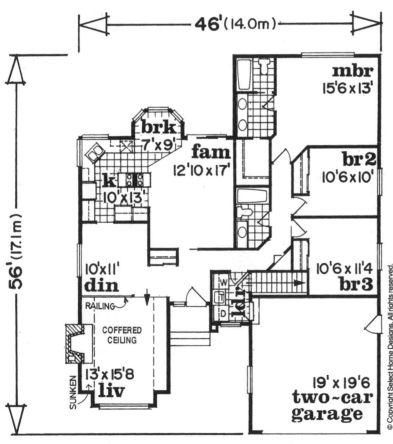

46' (14.0m)

56' (17.1m)

mbr
15'6 x 13'

brk
7' x 9'

fam
12'10 x 17'

br2
10'6 x 10'

k
10' x 13'

din
10' x 11'

RAILING

br3
10'6 x 11'4

liv
13' x 15'8

SUNKEN

COFFERED CEILING

W
D

two~car garage
19' x 19'6

floor plan   1650 sq.ft.

Features

- Design may be finished in either brick, siding or stucco.
- Roof line and windows differ with each elevation.
- Sunken living room, with masonry fireplace, is separated from dining room by low railing.
- Kitchen, with centre cooking island, serves breakfast bay.
- Large family room has sliding glass walk-through to patio.
- Master bedroom features walk-in closet and three-piece ensuite, with twin vanity and separate toilet and shower.

Total Living Area   1,650 sq. ft.

PRICE CODE: B

PLAN JA5459

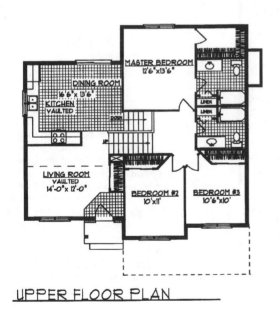

UPPER FLOOR PLAN

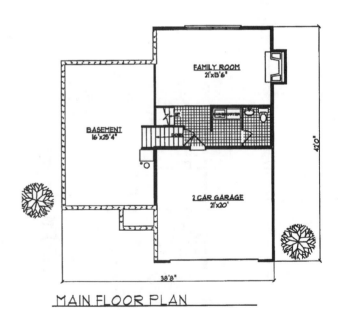

MAIN FLOOR PLAN

First Floor	449 sq. ft.
Second Floor	1,214 sq. ft.
Total Living Area	1,663 sq. ft.

PRICE CODE: B

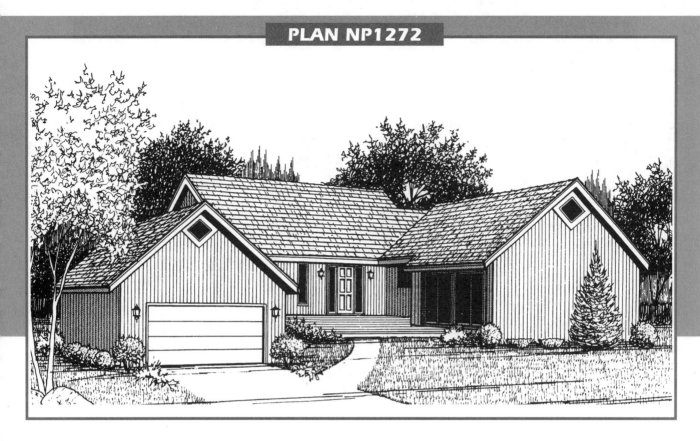

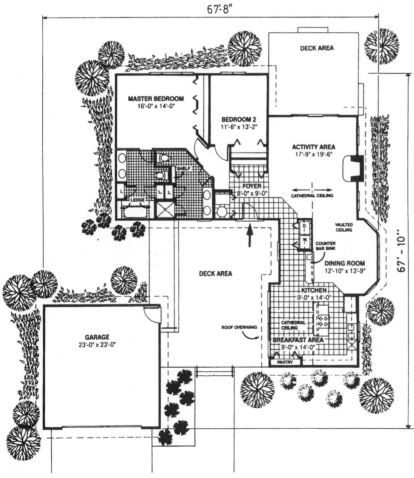

La Casa

Features

- L-Shaped contemporary home designed for smaller families.
- Foyer opens to activity area with cathedral ceiling and fireplace.
- Open kitchen design features pantry and large breakfast area with cathedral ceiling.
- Unique dining area features vaulted ceiling, bay windows, and open bar.
- Master bedroom includes a large bath with raised tub and shower area.
- Second bedroom also with dual-vanity and shower.

Total Living Area   **1,684 sq. ft.**

PRICE CODE: B

62

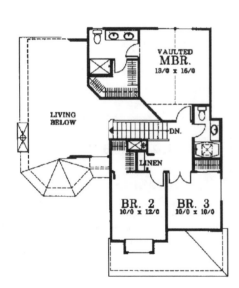

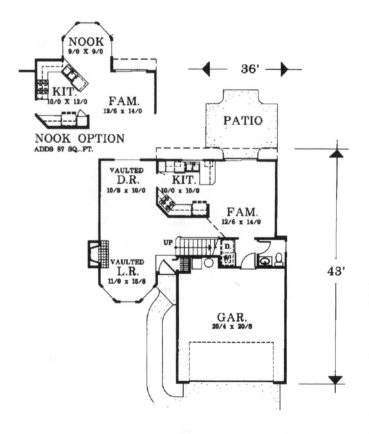

NOOK
9/0 X 9/0

KIT.
10/0 X 12/0

FAM.
12/6 x 14/0

NOOK OPTION
ADDS 87 SQ. FT.

36'

PATIO

VAULTED
D.R.
10/8 x 10/0

KIT.
10/0 x 10/0

FAM.
12/6 x 14/0

VAULTED
L.R.
11/0 x 15/8

UP

GAR.
20/4 x 20/8

43'

VAULTED
MBR.
13/8 x 15/0

LIVING
BELOW

DN.

LINEN

BR. 2
10/0 x 12/0

BR. 3
10/0 x 10/0

First Floor	748 sq. ft.
Second Floor	720 sq. ft.
Total Living Area	1,686 sq. ft.

PRICE CODE: B

BR. 3
11/10 X 10/0

BR. 2
11/10 X 10/6

DN

VAULTED
MASTER
13/0 X 14/8 +/-

SPA

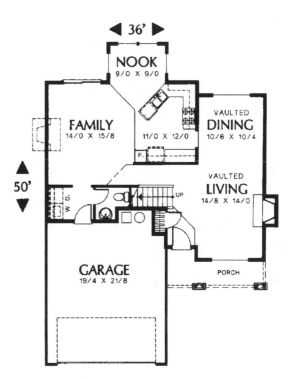

◀ 36' ▶

NOOK
9/0 X 9/0

FAMILY
14/0 X 15/8

11/0 X 12/0

VAULTED
DINING
10/6 X 10/4

50'

P.

VAULTED
LIVING
14/8 X 14/0

W. D.

UP

GARAGE
19/4 X 21/8

PORCH

First Floor	913 sq. ft.
Second Floor	813 sq. ft.
Total Living Area	1,726 sq. ft.

PRICE CODE: B

64

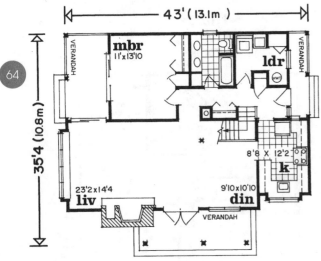

43' (13.1m)

35'4 (10.8m)

mbr
11'x13'10

ldr

HW'T

VERANDAH

VERANDAH

8'8 X 12'2

k

23'2 x14'4
liv

9'10x10'10
din

VERANDAH

First Level 1110 square feet

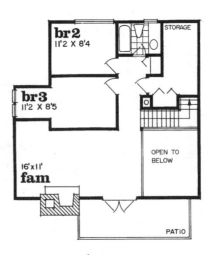

br2
11'2 X 8'4

STORAGE

br3
11'2 X 8'5

OPEN TO
BELOW

16'x11'
fam

PATIO

Second Level 625 square feet

Features

- French doors from the covered verandah open to a spacious living room and vaulted dining room.
- Masonry fireplace, with wood storage bin, warms this area.
- Sliding glass doors from the rear verandah open to the living room and master bedroom.
- Back door has easy access to a laundry / mud room.
- Family room, with fireplace and private deck, overlooks the dining room.
- Ample storage in the second level provides an additional 105 square feet.

Dining and living room with balcony over

Total Living Area   1,735 sq.

PRICE CODE: B

PLAN JA5359

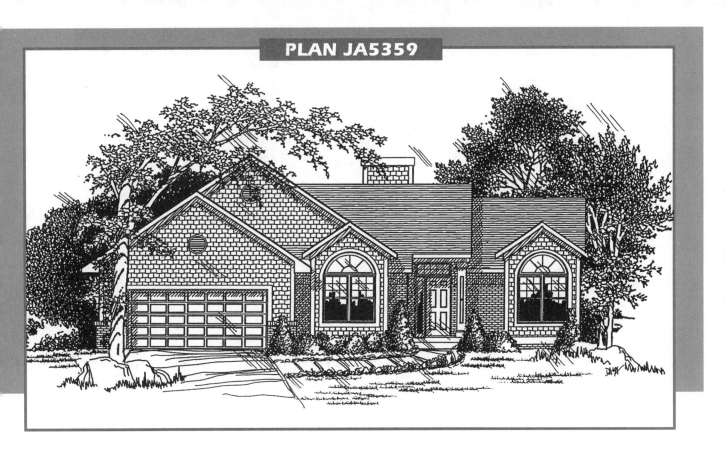

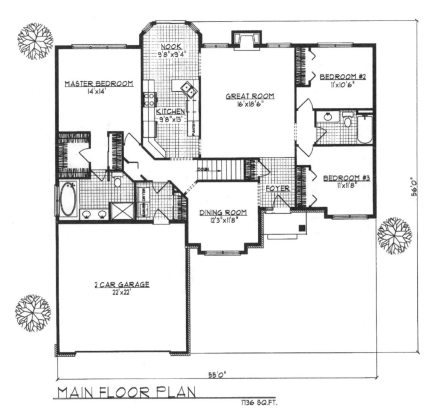

MAIN FLOOR PLAN

1136 SQ.FT.

- MASTER BEDROOM 14'x14'
- NOOK 9'8"x9'4"
- KITCHEN 9'8"x13'
- GREAT ROOM 16'x18'6"
- BEDROOM #2 11'x10'6"
- BEDROOM #3 11'x11'8"
- FOYER
- DINING ROOM 12'3"x11'8"
- 2 CAR GARAGE 22'x22'

55'0"

56'0"

65.

Total Living Area   **1,736 sq. ft.**

PRICE CODE: B

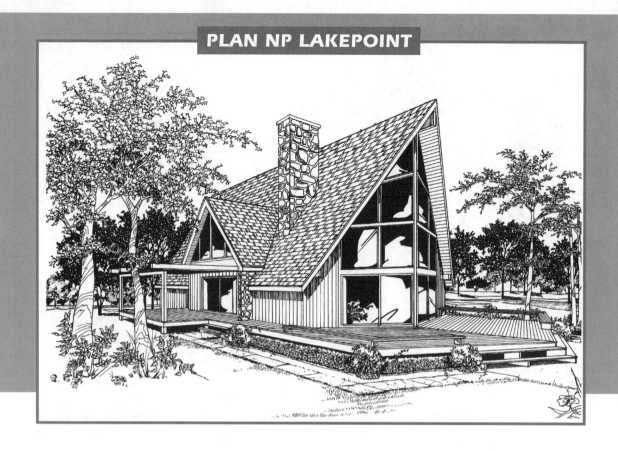

PLAN NP LAKEPOINT

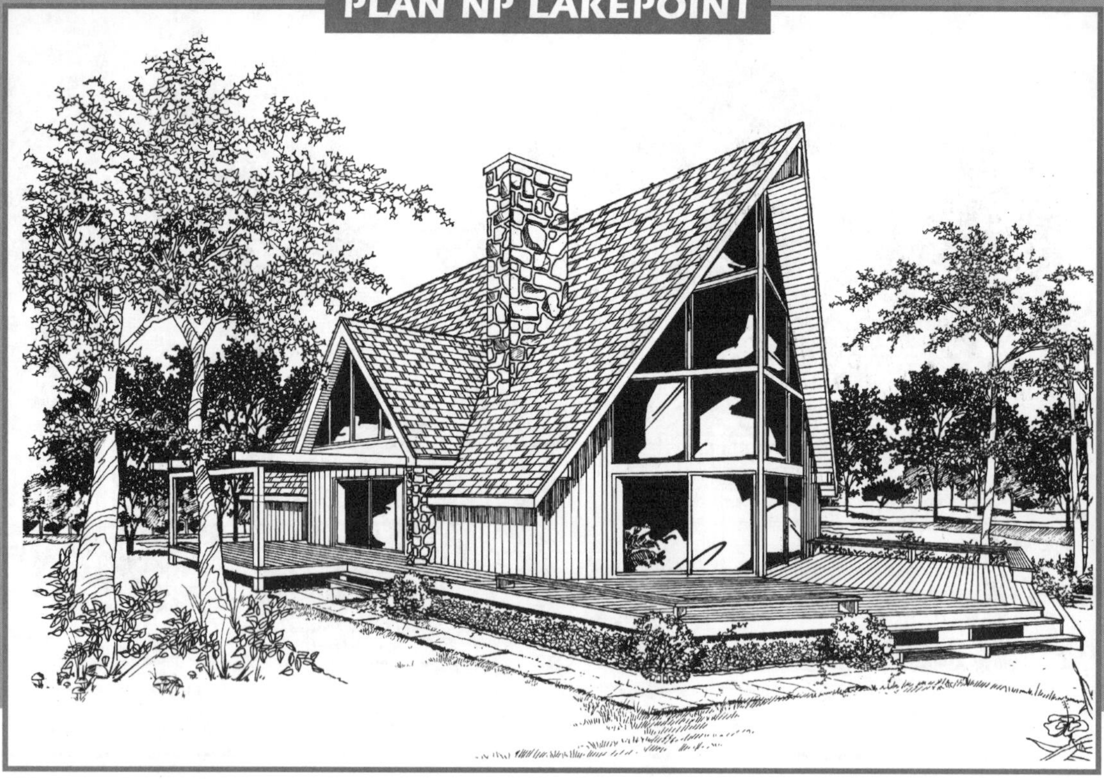

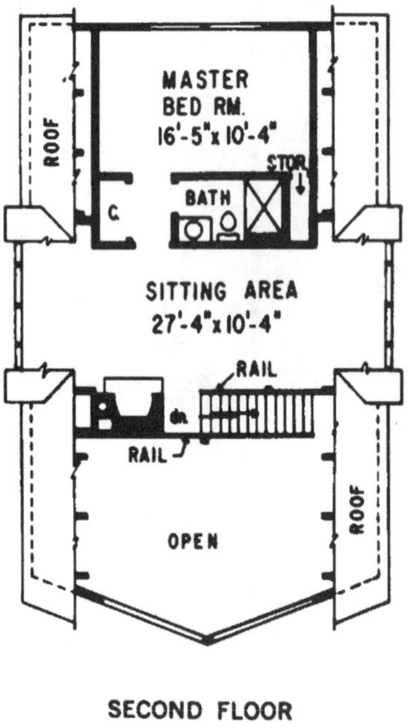
MASTER
BED RM.
16'-5"x 10'-4"
ROOF
STOR
BATH
C.
SITTING AREA
27'-4"x 10'-4"
RAIL
RAIL
OPEN
ROOF

SECOND FLOOR

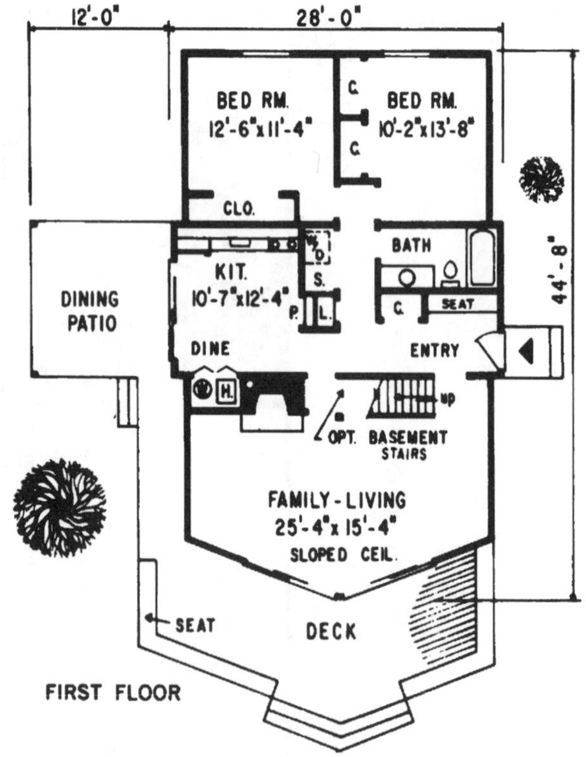
12'-0"
28'-0"
BED RM.
12'-6"x 11'-4"
BED RM.
10'-2"x 13'-8"
C.
C.
CLO.
KIT.
10'-7"x 12'-4"
BATH
DINING
PATIO
S.
P.
L.
C.
SEAT
44'-8"
DINE
ENTRY
H.
UP
OPT. BASEMENT
STAIRS
FAMILY-LIVING
25'-4"x 15'-4"
SLOPED CEIL.
SEAT
DECK

FIRST FLOOR

First Floor	1,126 sq. ft.
Second Floor	624 sq. ft.
Total Living Area	1,750 sq. ft.

PRICE CODE: B

Exterior view of Rear Elevation

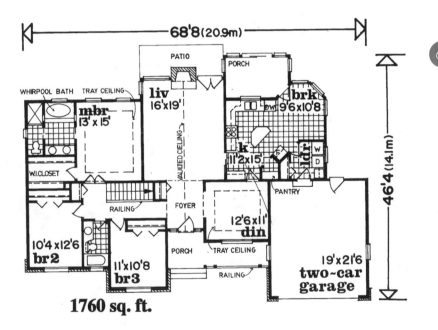

1760 sq. ft.

67

Features

- Covered, railed porch provides a weather-protected entry and introduces the vaulted foyer.
- Vaulted ceiling, extending from the foyer through to the living room, increases the sense of spaciousness.
- Floor plan is designed for a home with a view to the rear of the lot.
- Tray ceiling adds distinction and creates a formal atmosphere for the dining room.
- Open-plan kitchen includes a walk-in pantry, centre preparation island and breakfast bay.
- Windows surrounding the sunroom capture the sun's heat and warm this area.
- Master bedroom boasts a tray ceiling, walk-in closet and lavish ensuite with twin vanity, whirlpool spa and private plan shower.

Total Living Area   1,760 sq. ft.

PRICE CODE: B

PLAN MN1787

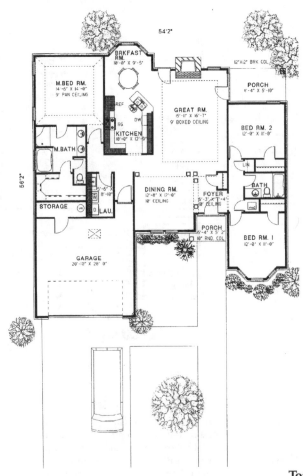

54'2"

BRKFAST RM.
10'-0" X 9'-5"

M.BED RM.
14'-6" X 14'-0"
9' PAN CEILING

12"X12" BRK COL

PORCH
11'-4" X 5'-10"

GREAT RM.
15'-11" X 16'-7"
9' BOXED CEILING

REF

RG

DW

KITCHEN
10'-0" X 12'-0"

BED RM. 2
12'-0" X 11'-0"

M.BATH

56'2"

LIN

BATH

DINING RM.
12'-8" X 12'-0"
10' CEILING

FOYER
15'-3" X 1'-4"
10' CEILING

STORAGE

LAU.

5'-6" X
8'-10"

PORCH
10'-4" X 5'-2"
10" RND. COL.

BED RM. 1
12'-0" X 11'-0"

GARAGE
20'-10" X 20'-0"

Total Living Area   1,787 sq. f

CUSTOMIZE IT!

ORDER TOLL FREE   1▪800▪533▪4350   24-HOUR FAX ORDERING   1▪800▪344▪4293

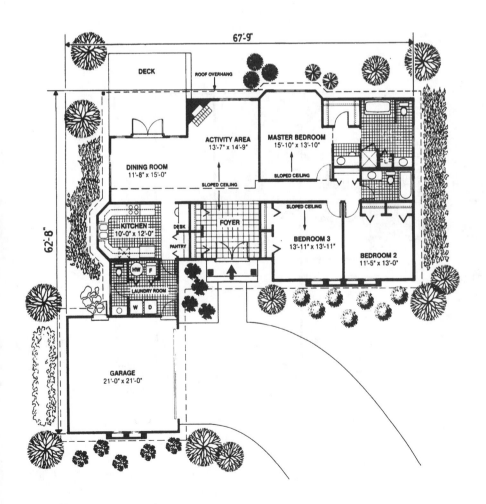

DECK

ROOF OVERHANG

67'-9"

62'-8"

ACTIVITY AREA
13'-7" x 14'-9"

MASTER BEDROOM
15'-10" x 13'-10"

DINING ROOM
11'-8" x 15'-0"

SLOPED CEILING

SLOPED CEILING

KITCHEN
10'-0" x 12'-0"

DESK

FOYER

PANTRY

SLOPED CEILING

BEDROOM 3
13'-11" x 13'-11"

HW   F

LAUNDRY ROOM

W   D

BEDROOM 2
11'-5" x 13'-0"

GARAGE
21'-0" x 21'-0"

69

Casual Ranch

Features

- Comforts abound in this well-designed ranch.
- Sunlit entryway leads to activity area with corner fireplace at rear of home.
- U-shaped kitchen with built-in pantry and desk is adjacent to dining room with optional deck.
- Large laundry area/powder room conveniently located adjacent to garage, just off kitchen.
- Master bedroom features large, walk-in closet, dressing area with make-up vanity, and compartmented master bath with shower and raised tub.
- Two additional bedrooms are served with a full bath.

Total Living Area   1,800 sq. ft.

PRICE CODE: B

PLAN JA5219

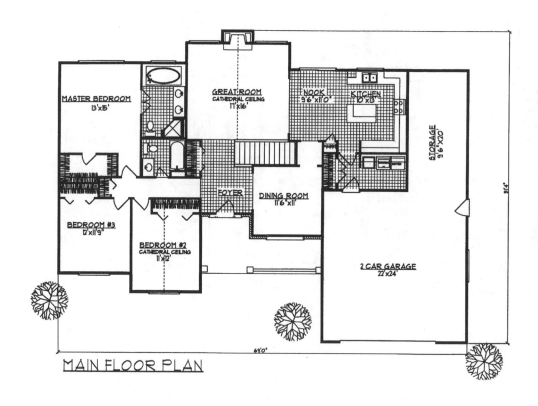

MASTER BEDROOM 13'x15'

GREAT ROOM CATHEDRAL CEILING 17'x16'

NOOK 9'6"x11'0"

KITCHEN 10'x13'

STORAGE 9'6"x20'

FOYER

DINING ROOM 11'6"x11'

BEDROOM #3 12'x11'9"

BEDROOM #2 CATHEDRAL CEILING 11'x12'

2 CAR GARAGE 22'x24'

57'4"

69'0"

MAIN FLOOR PLAN

Total Living Area 1,802 sq. f

71

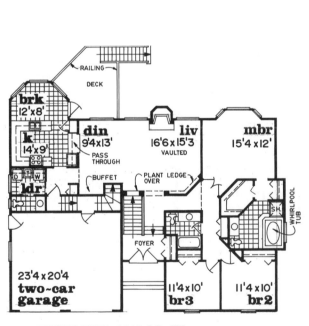

FIRST LEVEL 1816 SQ. FT.

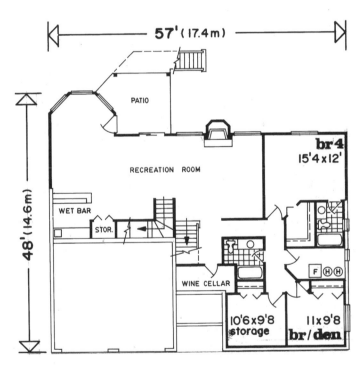

LOWER LEVEL

Features

- Design ideal for a lot that slopes to the rear; rooms positioned to capture the view to the rear of the home.
- Skylit foyer, with plant ledge over, steps up to spacious living and dining room.
- Efficient U-plan shaped kitchen, with breakfast bay, has a pass through to the dining room.
- Master bedroom boasts a walk-in and wall closet, and ensuite with raised whirlpool spa.
- Expansive recreation or game room, with wet bar, bay window sitting area, fireplace and covered patio, has two stairway accesses.
- Fourth bedroom has a walk-in closet and three-piece ensuite.
- Unfinished lower level offers potential for an additonal 1,725 square feet.

Total Living Area   1,816 sq. ft.

PRICE CODE: B

CUSTOMIZE IT!

ORDER TOLL FREE   1 ▪ 800 ▪ 533 ▪ 4350   24-HOUR FAX ORDERING   1 ▪ 800 ▪ 344 ▪ 4293

PLAN MN1817

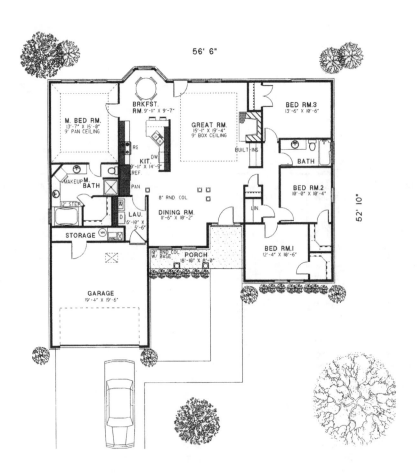

56' 6"

52' 10"

M. BED RM.
13'-7" X 15'-0"
9' PAN CEILING

BRKFST.
RM. 9'-11" X 9'-7"

GREAT RM.
15'-1" X 19'-4"
9' BOX CEILING

BED RM.3
13'-6" X 10'-6"

BUILT-INS

BATH

KIT.
9'-11" X 14'-0"

REF.

MAKEUP M.
BATH

PAN

8" RND COL.

LIN.

BED RM.2
10'-0" X 10'-4"

12" STER.

LAU.
6'-10" X
5'-6"

DINING RM.
11'-6" X 10'-2"

STORAGE

WIN

10" RND. COL.
W/ BASE

PORCH
16'-10" X 8'-0"

BED RM.1
12'-4" X 10'-6"

GARAGE
19'-4" X 19'-6"

Total Living Area   1,817 sq. ft

PRICE CODE: B

CUSTOMIZE IT!

ORDER TOLL FREE   1 ▪ 800 ▪ 533 ▪ 4350   **24-HOUR FAX ORDERING**   1 ▪ 800 ▪ 344 ▪ 4293

◀ 36' ▶

▲ 33' ▼

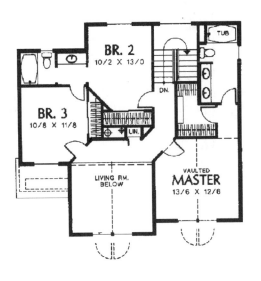

BR. 2
10/2 X 13/0

TUB

BR. 3
10/8 X 11/8

DN.

LIN.

LIVING RM.
BELOW

VAULTED
MASTER
13/6 X 12/6

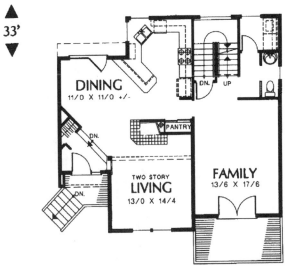

DINING
11/0 X 11/0 +/-

DN.   UP

PANTRY

DN.

TWO STORY
LIVING
13/0 X 14/4

FAMILY
13/6 X 17/6

DN.

TWO CAR GARAGE BELOW

First Floor	1,022 sq. ft.
Second Floor	813 sq. ft.
Total Living Area	1,835 sq. ft.

PRICE CODE: B

CUSTOMIZE IT!

ORDER TOLL FREE   1 ▪ 800 ▪ 533 ▪ 4350   24-HOUR FAX ORDERING   1 ▪ 800 ▪ 344 ▪ 4293

74

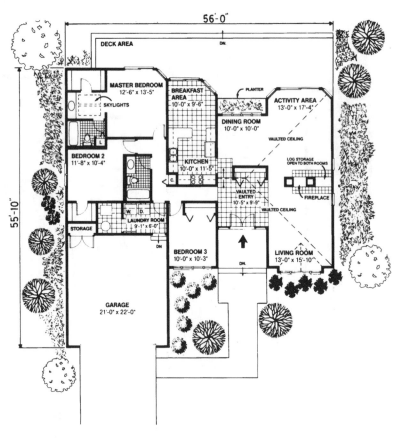

DECK AREA

56'-0"

DN.

MASTER BEDROOM
12'-6" x 13'-5"

SKYLIGHTS

BREAKFAST AREA
10'-0" x 9'-6"

PLANTER

ACTIVITY AREA
13'-0" x 17'-4"

DINING ROOM
10'-0" x 10'-0"

VAULTED CEILING

BEDROOM 2
11'-8" x 10'-4"

KITCHEN
10'-0" x 11'-5"

LOG STORAGE
OPEN TO BOTH ROOMS

VAULTED ENTRY
10'-5" x 9'-9"

FIREPLACE

55'-10"

W. D.

LAUNDRY ROOM
9'-1" x 6'-0"

VAULTED CEILING

STORAGE

DN.

BEDROOM 3
10'-0" x 10'-3"

DN.

LIVING ROOM
13'-0" x 15'-10"

GARAGE
21'-0" x 22'-0"

Total Living Area   1,850 sq. ft.

PRICE CODE: B

CUSTOMIZE IT!

ORDER TOLL FREE   1▪800▪533▪4350   24-HOUR FAX ORDERING   1▪800▪344▪4293

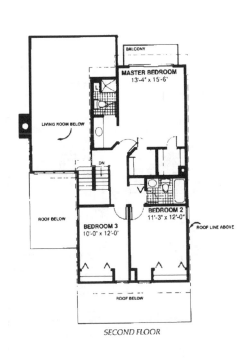

SECOND FLOOR

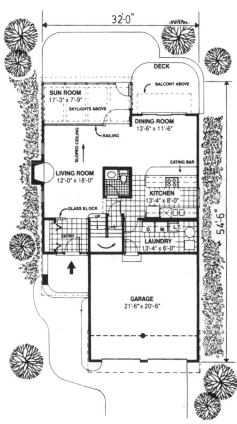

Hidden Treasures

Features

- Perfect for a narrow lot.
- Spacious, comfortable design.
- Sloped ceilings crown entry and living room.
- Dining room adjoins kitchen with breakfast bar.
- Sunken sun room with skylights is delightful retreat or perfect for entertaining.

- Optional multi-level wooden deck can be accessed either from sun room or dining room.
- Two bedrooms with bath and master bedroom with private bath upstairs.
- Balcony off master bedroom overlooks living room.

First Floor	896 sq. ft.
Second Floor	977 sq. ft.
Total Living Area	1,873 sq. ft.

PRICE CODE: B

CUSTOMIZE IT!

ORDER TOLL FREE **1■800■533■4350** 24-HOUR FAX ORDERING **1■800■344■4293**

76

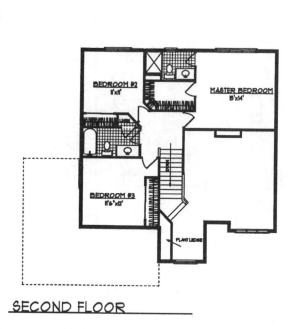

SECOND FLOOR

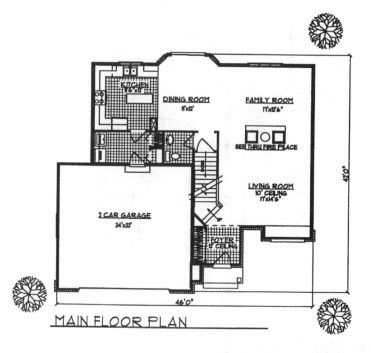

MAIN FLOOR PLAN

First Floor	1,080 sq. ft.
Second Floor	794 sq. ft.
Total Living Area	1,874 sq. ft.

PRICE CODE: B

CUSTOMIZE IT!

ORDER TOLL FREE **1 ▪ 800 ▪ 533 ▪ 4350**   24-HOUR FAX ORDERING   **1 ▪ 800 ▪ 344 ▪ 4293**

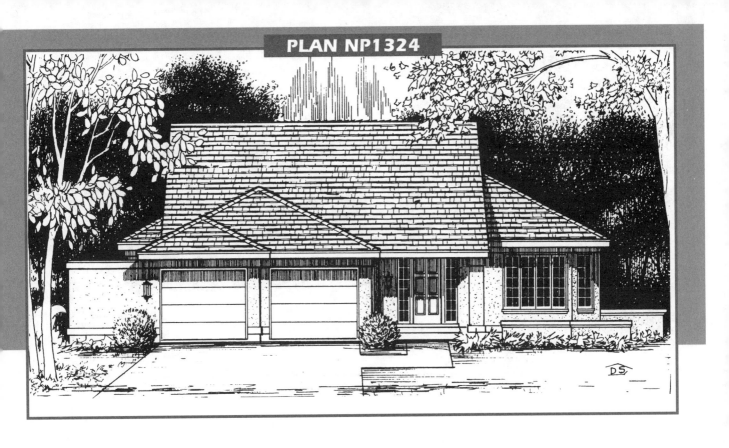

PLAN NP1324

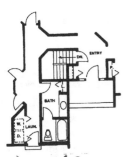

Plan 1 with Basement

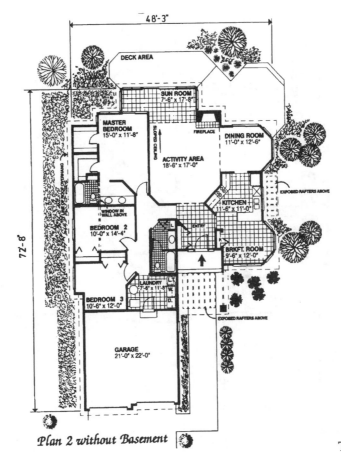

Plan 2 without Basement

Eastwind

Features

- Handsome, contemporary design marks this home as special.
- Entry foyer opens to kitchen and breakfast area on the right and a large activity area on the left.
- Activity area amenities include a fireplace and sun room.
- Formal dining area with bay windows and sliding glass doors located at rear of kitchen.
- Master bedroom has his/her walk-in closets and a dual-vanity bath.
- Two additional bedrooms share one full bath.

Total Living Area   1,907 sq. ft.

PRICE CODE: B

CUSTOMIZE IT!

ORDER TOLL FREE   1•800•533•4350   24-HOUR FAX ORDERING   1•800•344•4293

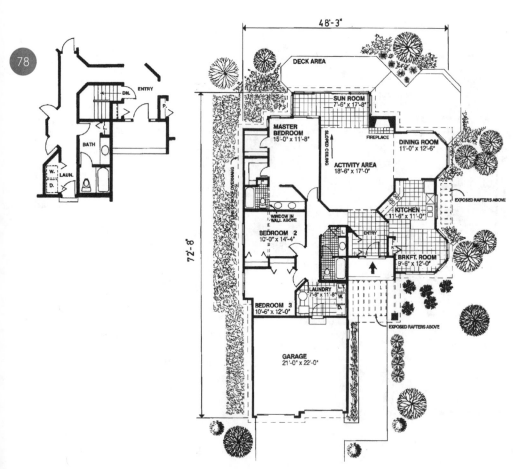

78

Arboure Wood

Features

- Exposed entry rafters, wide overhanging gable roof lines, and vertical windows combine to make this home smartly elegant.
- Activity area with fireplace opens to dining room.
- Sun room off activity area leads to deck.
- Laundry room conveniently located in bedroom wing of home.
- Two bedrooms share a full bath.
- Additional master bedroom suite features access to the sun room plus a deluxe master bath with clerestory window and large closets.

Total Living Area   1,907 sq. ft.

PRICE CODE: B

79

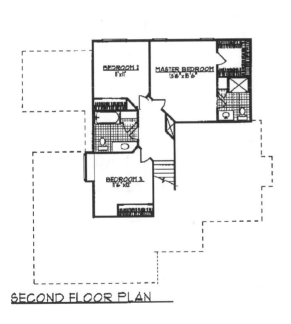

SECOND FLOOR PLAN

FIRST FLOOR PLAN

First Floor	1,132 sq. ft.
Second Floor	797 sq. ft.
Total Living Area	1,929 sq. ft.

PRICE CODE: B

80

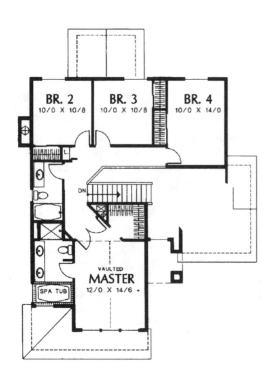

BR. 2
10/0 X 10/8

BR. 3
10/0 X 10/8

BR. 4
10/0 X 14/0

DN

VAULTED
MASTER
12/0 X 14/6 +

SPA TUB

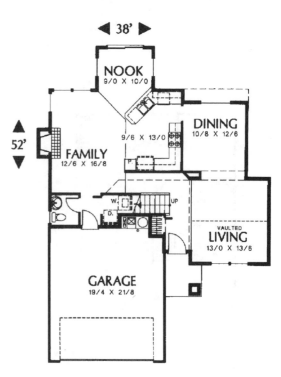

◄ 38' ►

NOOK
9/0 X 10/0

52'

FAMILY
12/6 X 16/8

9/6 X 13/0

DINING
10/8 X 12/6

W.

UP

VAULTED
LIVING
13/0 X 13/6

GARAGE
19/4 X 21/8

First Floor	960 sq. ft.
Second Floor	968 sq. ft.
Total Living Area	1,928 sq. ft.

PRICE CODE: B

50-6

60-9

Total Living Area   **1,941 sq. ft.**

PRICE CODE: B

CUSTOMIZE IT!

ORDER TOLL FREE   1▪800▪533▪4350   24-HOUR FAX ORDERING   1▪800▪344▪4293

◀ **40'** ▶

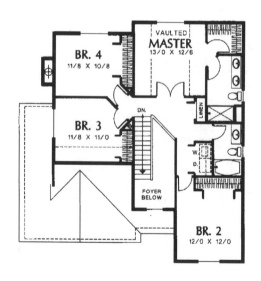

▲
42'
▼

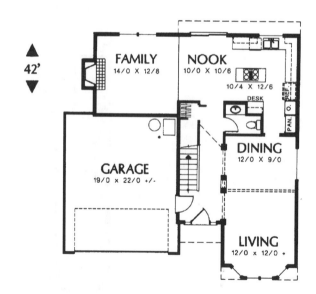

82

First Floor	944 sq. ft.
Second Floor	1,013 sq. ft.
Total Living Area	1,957 sq. ft.

PRICE CODE: B

PLAN MN1963

83

Total Living Area 1,963 sq. ft.

PRICE CODE: B

84

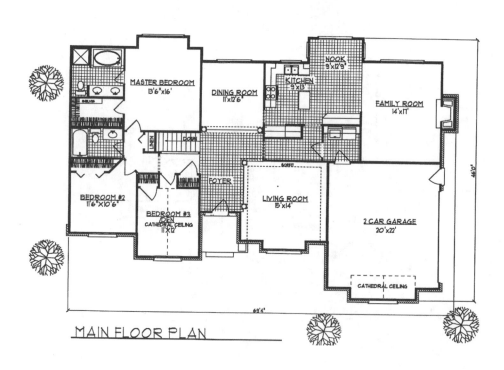

MAIN FLOOR PLAN

Total Living Area   1,984 sq. ft.

PRICE CODE: B

85

Total Living Area   **1,987 sq. ft.**

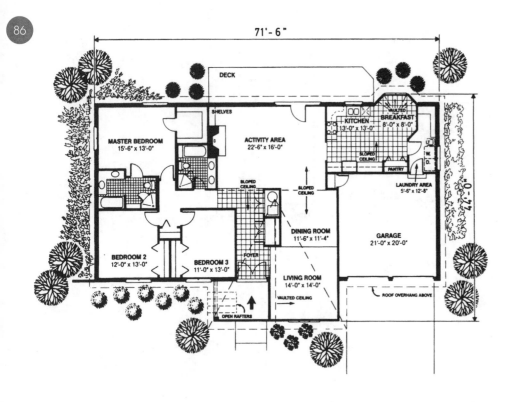

71'- 6 "

DECK

SHELVES

MASTER BEDROOM
15'-6" x 13'-0"

ACTIVITY AREA
22'-6" x 16'-0"

KITCHEN
13'-0" x 13'-0"

VAULTED
BREAKFAST
8'-0" x 8'-0"

SLOPED
CEILING

PANTRY

SLOPED
CEILING

LAUNDRY AREA
5'-6" x 12'-8"

W.
D.

SLOPED
CEILING

DINING ROOM
11'-6" x 11'-4"

GARAGE
21'-0" x 20'-0"

BEDROOM 2
12'-0" x 13'-0"

BEDROOM 3
11'-0" x 13'-0"

FOYER

LIVING ROOM
14'-0" x 14'-0"

VAULTED CEILING

ROOF OVERHANG ABOVE

OPEN RAFTERS

Ranch Castille

Features

- A practical design with an attractive, arched main entrance mark this home as something special.
- Left wing includes master bedroom with walk-in closet and bathroom suite.
- Two additional bedroom in the left wing share a full bath with both tub and shower.
- Right wing features a living room with vaulted ceiling, and a dining room and activity room with sloped ceilings for added interest.
- Kitchen is tucked away at the left rear and includes sloped ceiling and built-in pantry.
- Vaulted breakfast nook includes bay window.
- Large deck off activity area for expanding your entertaining options.

Total Living Area   **1,990 sq. ft.**

PRICE CODE: B

PLAN JA5269

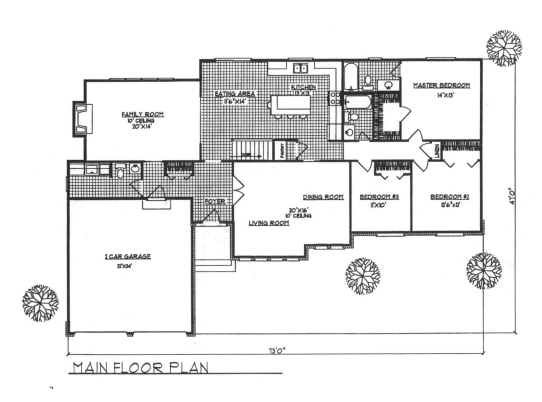

MAIN FLOOR PLAN

FAMILY ROOM
10' CEILING
20'X14'

EATING AREA
11'6"X14'

KITCHEN
13'X13'

MASTER BEDROOM
14'X13'

2 CAR GARAGE
22'X24'

FOYER

DINING ROOM

LIVING ROOM
20'X16'
10' CEILING

BEDROOM #3
11'X10'

BEDROOM #2
12'6"X12'

LINEN

PANTRY

73'0"

41'0"

Total Living Area   2,042 sq. ft.

PRICE CODE: B

CUSTOMIZE IT!

ORDER TOLL FREE   1▪800▪533▪4350   24-HOUR FAX ORDERING   1▪800▪344▪4293

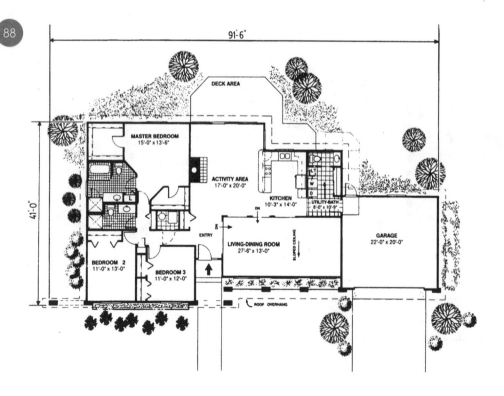

Spanish Ranch

Features

- Spanish facade with raised planters, Spanish-clay roofing, and exposed rafters make this ranch-style home extra charming.
- Inside, comfort is the key.
- Entrance leads to sloped-ceiling, sunken living/dining room on the right.
- Activity area at the rear of the home includes a fireplace and snack bar.
- U-shaped kitchen is accessed from the garage.
- Left-wing sleeping quarters include a master bedroom with private bath featuring raised tub and shower and two additional bedrooms with full bath.

Total Living Area **2,050 sq. ft.**

PRICE CODE: B

60'-0"

57'-1"

Covered Patio

MstrBed
15x14
Sloped Clg.
8'-0" to 11'-0"

GreatRm
18x17
9'-0" Clg/rm

Brkfst
11x10
9'-0" Clg.

Bed#3
14x10
8'-0" Clg.

Kit
12x11
9'-0" Clg.

Gallery
9'-0" Clg.

Bed#2
10x13
8'-0" Clg.

Walk-in Closet
8'-0" Clg.

Pwdr

Util

Study
11x11
9'-0" Clg.

Ent

FmlDin
11x13
10'-0" Clg.

Por.

Gar
20x22
8'-4" Clg.

Stoop

Total Living Area   2,061 sq. ft.

PRICE CODE: B

C U S T O M I Z E   I T !

ORDER TOLL FREE 1 ▪ 800 ▪ 533 ▪ 4350   **24-HOUR FAX ORDERING** 1 ▪ 800 ▪ 344 ▪ 4293

PLAN FD8121-L

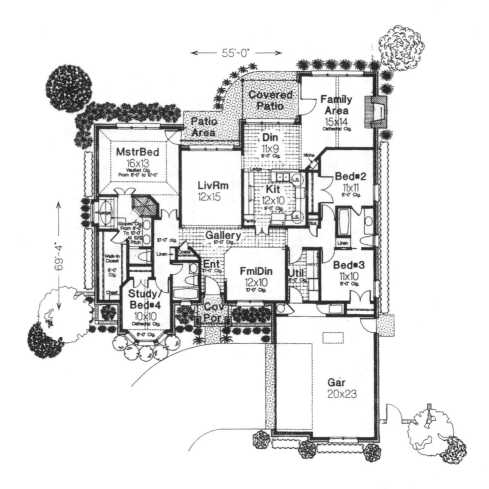

← 55'-0" →

69'-4"

Covered Patio

Patio Area

Family Area 15x14 Cathedral Clg.

MstrBed 16x13 Vaulted Clg. From 8'-0" to 10'-0"

Din 11x9 9'-0" Clg.

LivRm 12x15

Kit 12x10 9'-0" Clg.

Bed#2 11x11 8'-0" Clg.

Gallery 10'-0" Clg.

Ent 10'-0" Clg.

FmlDin 12x10 10'-0" Clg.

Util

Bed#3 11x10 8'-0" Clg.

Study/ Bed#4 10x10 Cathedral Clg. 8'-0" Clg.

Cov Por

Gar 20x23

Total Living Area   2,063 sq. ft

PRICE CODE: B

CUSTOMIZE IT!

ORDER TOLL FREE 1▪800▪533▪4350   24-HOUR FAX ORDERING 1▪800▪344▪4293

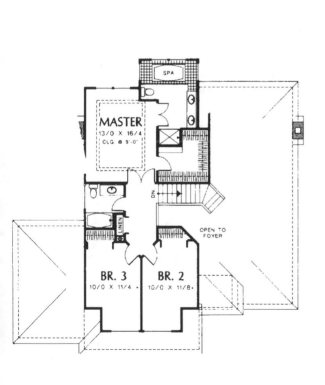

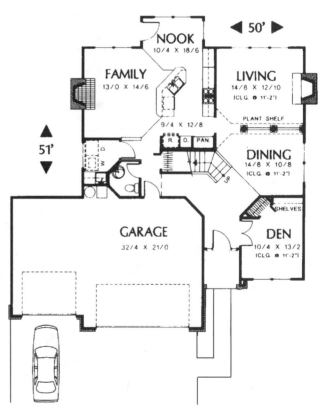

91

First Floor	1,186 sq. ft.
Second Floor	895 sq. ft.
Total Living Area	2,081 sq. ft.

PRICE CODE: B

PLAN NP1266

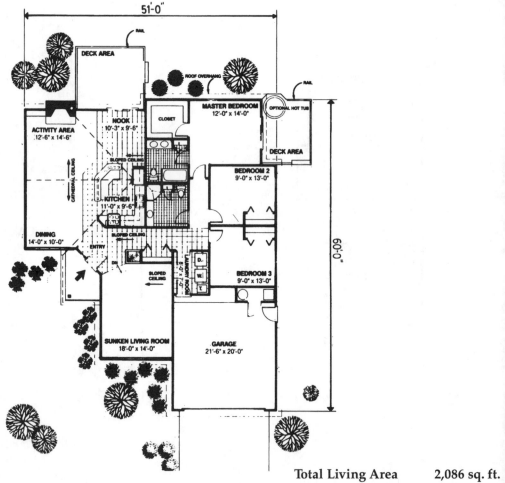

51'-0"

DECK AREA

RAIL

ROOF OVERHANG

RAIL

OPTIONAL HOT TUB

MASTER BEDROOM
12'-0" x 14'-0"

CLOSET

DECK AREA

NOOK
10'-3" x 9'-6"

ACTIVITY AREA
12'-6" x 14'-6"

BEDROOM 2
9'-0" x 13'-0"

SLOPED CEILING

CATHEDRAL CEILING

KITCHEN
11'-0" x 9'-6"

DINING
14'-0" x 10'-0"

SLOPED CEILING

ENTRY

LAUNDRY ROOM
8'-0" x 7'-0"

BEDROOM 3
9'-0" x 13'-0"

SLOPED CEILING

60'-0"

SUNKEN LIVING ROOM
18'-0" x 14'-0"

GARAGE
21'-6" x 20'-0"

Total Living Area   2,086 sq. ft.

PRICE CODE: B

PLAN JA5259

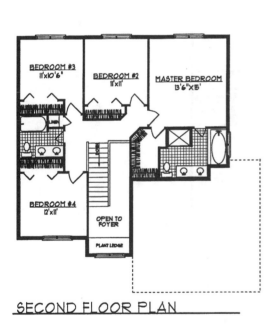

SECOND FLOOR PLAN

BEDROOM #3
11'x10'6"

BEDROOM #2
11'x11'

MASTER BEDROOM
13'6"x15'

BEDROOM #4
12'x11'

OPEN TO FOYER

PLANT LEDGE

MAIN FLOOR PLAN

93

NOOK
14'x9'6"

GREAT ROOM
22'x14'6"

KITCHEN
14'x11'6"

DINING ROOM
12'x12'6"

FOYER

2 CAR GARAGE
20'x22'

44'0"

40'8"

First Floor	1,102 sq. ft.
Second Floor	1,004 sq. ft.
Total Living Area	2,106 sq. ft.

PRICE CODE: B

PLAN MN2107

64' 8"

PATIO
31'-8" X 17'-0"

12" BRK COL

PORCH

BED RM. 3
14'-4" X 11'-0"

BRKFST. RM.
12'-6" X 9'-2"

M. BATH

M. BED RM.
15'-8" X 14'-0"
9' PAN CEILING

LAUNDRY
7'-6" X 6'-0"

BATH

GREAT RM.
19'-6" X 17'-4"
10' CEILING

REF.
PAN

KITCHEN
12'-6" X 10'-2"
OVEN

BATH

STOR.
7'-6" X 4'-5"

LIN

BATH

LIN

62' 1"

DW

CT

BUILT-IN
W/ CAB.

BED RM. 1
10'-6" X 12'-0"

FOYER
6'-4" X 7'-8"
10' CEILING

8' CEILING

GARAGE
20' 4" X 24' 6"

BED RM. 2
11'-0" X 12'-0"

DINING RM.
11'-0" X 12'-0"
9' BOX CEILING

12" BRK COL

PORCH
7'-8" X 6'-9"

PLANTER

Total Living Area 2,107 sq.

94

PLAN FD8028B

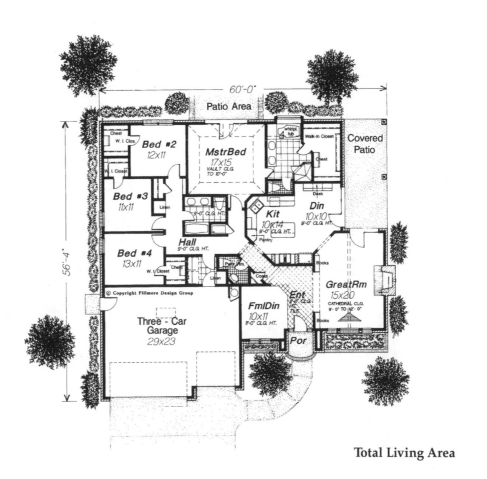

Total Living Area 2,118 sq. ft.

PRICE CODE: B

PLAN SH90-2173

96

basement stair location

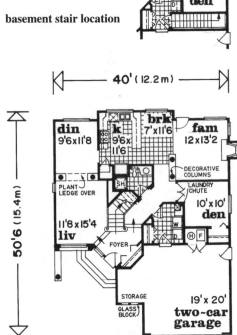

den

WHIRLPOOL
TUB

SH

mbr
15' x 13'

LAUNDRY
CHUTE

PLANT LEDGE

OPEN TO
FOYER BELOW

9'4 x 10'
br3

9'4 x 10'
br2

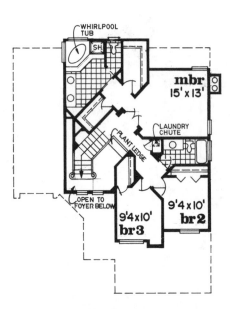

Second Level 921 sq. ft.

40' (12.2 m)

50'6 (15.4 m)

din
9'6x11'8

k
9'6x
11'6

brk
7'x11'6

fam
12 x 13'2

PLANT
LEDGE OVER

SH

DECORATIVE
COLUMNS

LAUNDRY
CHUTE

11'8 x 15'4
liv

FOYER

W

10'x 10'
den

H F

STORAGE

GLASS
BLOCK

19' x 20'
two~car
garage

First Level 1199 sq. ft

Features

- Tall multipaned window walls accentuate the two storey entry and the high ceiling in the living room.
- Pair of decorative columns, with planter ledge over, provides visual separation of the living and dining room.
- U-plan shaped kitchen, with walk-in pantry and abundant counter space, serves the break-

fast area.
- Laundry chute from the second level eases household chores.
- Master bedroom boasts his and hers walk-in closets and ensuite with raised spa.
- Plan includes a basement and crawlspace foundation.

Total Living Area   2,120 sq. f

PRICE CODE: B

PLAN FD8023

97

Total Living Area   2,124 sq. ft.

PRICE CODE: B

98

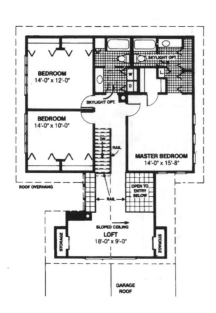

First Floor

Lofty Ideals

Features

- This two-story home features a front-facing loft and balcony for extra appeal.
- Large, tiled entryway leads to living room and activity room, which share a two-way fireplace.
- Three optional deck areas with planters extend the living/entertaining possibilities.

- Skylights brighten both the compartmented hall bath and master bath.
- Second- floor master bedroom features include sloped ceilings and walk-in closet.
- Loft, 230 square feet.

First Floor	1,129 sq. ft.
Second Floor	1,008 sq. ft.
Loft	230 sq. ft.
Total Living Area	2,367 sq. ft.

PRICE CODE: C

PLAN JA5279

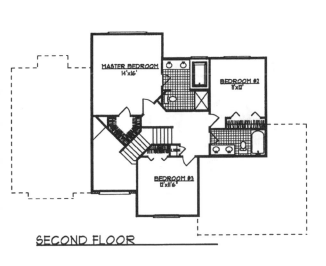

SECOND FLOOR

MASTER BEDROOM
14'x16'

BEDROOM #2
11'x12'

BEDROOM #3
12'x11'6"

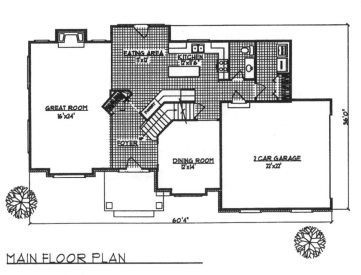

MAIN FLOOR PLAN

EATING AREA
11'x12'

KITCHEN
12'x11'6"

GREAT ROOM
16'x24'

FOYER

DINING ROOM
12'x14'

2 CAR GARAGE
22'x22'

36'0"

60'4"

First Floor	1,253 sq. ft.
Second Floor	885 sq. ft.
Total Living Area	2,138 sq. ft.

PRICE CODE: B

CUSTOMIZE IT!

ORDER TOLL FREE   **1▪800▪533▪4350**   **24-HOUR FAX ORDERING**   **1▪800▪344▪4293**

PLAN FD7663-LB

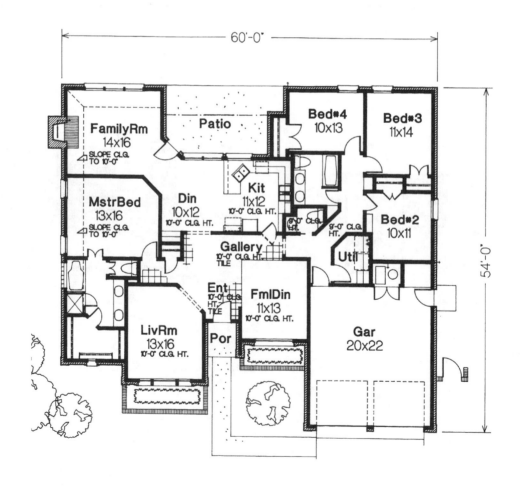

100

FamilyRm 14x16
SLOPE CLG. TO 10'-0"

Patio

Bed#4 10x13

Bed#3 11x14

MstrBed 13x16
SLOPE CLG. TO 10'-0"

Din 10x12
10'-0" CLG. HT.

Kit 11x12
10'-0" CLG. HT.

Bed#2 10x11

9'-0" CLG. HT.

Gallery
10'-0" CLG. HT.
TILE

Util

Ent
10'-0" CLG. HT.
TILE

FmlDin 11x13
10'-0" CLG. HT.

LivRm 13x16
10'-0" CLG. HT.

Por

Gar 20x22

60'-0"

54'-0"

Total Living Area   2,140 sq. ft.

PLAN JA5179

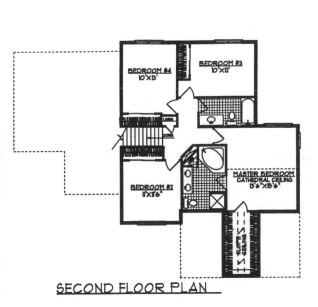

SECOND FLOOR PLAN

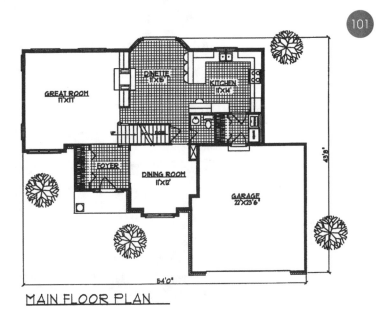

MAIN FLOOR PLAN

First Floor	1,086 sq. ft.
Second Floor	1,064 sq. ft.
Total Living Area	2,150 sq. ft.

PRICE CODE: B

CUSTOMIZE IT!

ORDER TOLL FREE 1•800•533•4350   24-HOUR FAX ORDERING 1•800•344•4293

102

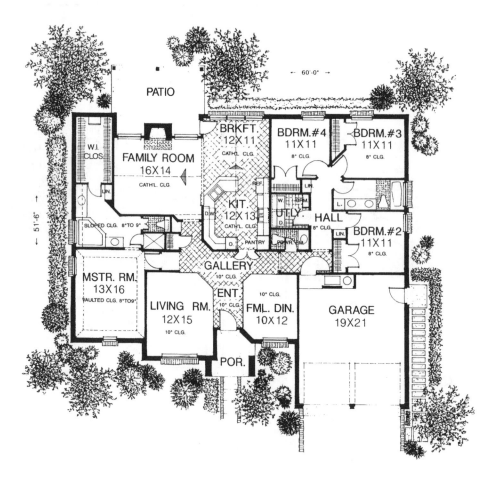

PATIO

W.I. CLOS.

FAMILY ROOM
16X14
CATH'L. CLG.

BRKFT.
12X11
CATH'L. CLG.

BDRM.#4
11X11
8° CLG.

BDRM.#3
11X11
8° CLG.

REF.

LIN.

KIT.
12X13
CATH'L. CLG.

W

DRM.

HALL
8° CLG.

LIN.

DW

UTL.
8° CLG.

D

BDRM.#2
11X11
8° CLG.

SLOPED CLG. 8°TO 9°

LIN.

O.

PANTRY

POWR. RM.

GALLERY
10° CLG.

MSTR. RM.
13X16
VAULTED CLG. 8°TO9°

LIVING RM.
12X15
10° CLG.

ENT.
10° CLG.

FML. DIN.
10X12
10° CLG.

GARAGE
19X21

POR.

60'-0"

51'-6"

Total Living Area   2,151 sq. ft.

CUSTOMIZE IT!

ORDER TOLL FREE   1■800■533■4350   24-HOUR FAX ORDERING   1■800■344■4293

DECK

62'-7"

ACTIVITY AREA
12'-0" x 17'-3"
VAULTED CEILING

BREAKFAST
8'-0" x 8'-0"

DINING ROOM
10'-0" x 15'-0"
VAULTED CEILING

MASTER BEDROOM
13'-0" x 20'-0"

KITCHEN
11'-3" x 15'-0"

BEDROOM 2
11'-3" x 11'-10"

LIVING ROOM
15'-0" x 15'-6"
VAULTED CEILING

ENTRY

62'-0"

BEDROOM 3
11'-6" x 11'-6"

LAUNDRY
6'-0" x 12'-3"

ROOF OVERHANG

GARAGE
21'-0" x 22'-0"

103

Vaulted Villa

Features

- Unique roof angles make this an eye-catching design.
- Foyer entrance angles to access living room, activity area, and dining room.
- Vaulted ceilings featured in the living room and activity room.
- Activity room also includes fireplace.
- Kitchen with center island opens to breakfast bay area and dining room.
- Master bedroom with bay windows includes a raised-tub master bath and two walk-in closets.
- Two additional bedrooms share full bath.

Total Living Area   **2,155 sq. ft.**

PRICE CODE: B

PLAN SH1989-2145

104

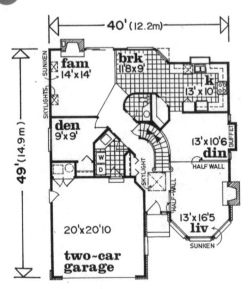

40' (12.2m)

49' (14.9 m)

SUNKEN / SKYLIGHTS

fam 14'x14'

brk 11'8x9'

k 13' x 10'

den 9'x9'

SKYLIGHT

13'x10'6 **din**

HALF WALL

HALF-WALL

W D

BUFFET

13' x 16'5 **liv**

SUNKEN

20'x20'10

two-car garage

first level 1227 sq. ft.

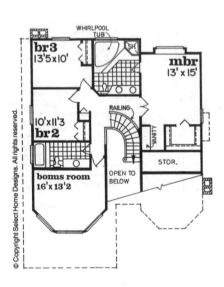

WHIRLPOOL TUB

br3 13'5x10'

SH

mbr 13' x 15'

RAILING

10'x11'3 **br2**

VANITY

bonus room 16'x13'2

OPEN TO BELOW

STOR.

second level 938 sq. ft.

Features

- Sweeping curved staircase dominates skylit foyer.
- Sunken living room rests in windowed bay.
- Half wall separates dining room from living room.
- Kitchen, with walk-in pantry and breakfast room, overlooks sunken family room.
- Skylights and sliding glass doors brighten family room.
- Master bedroom features a walk-in closet and ensuite, with whirlpool spa, twin vanity and shower.
- Bonus room, with expansive windows, provides 212 additional square feet.

Total Living Area	2,165 sq. ft

PRICE CODE: B

PLAN DB2328

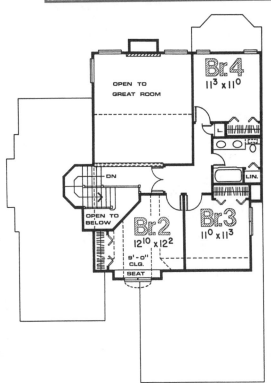

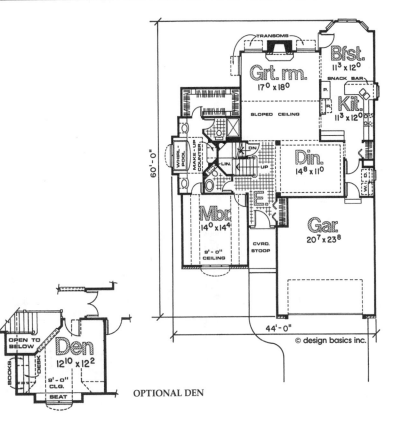

OPTIONAL DEN

Features

- Alluring brick elevation, openness of dining room enhanced by elegant columns.
- Great room with bright windows includes raised hearth fireplace.
- Kitchen and bayed breakfast area support leisure or entertaining activities.
- Second floor features optional den/loft with built-in desk and bookshelves.
- Bath with dual lavs serves secondary bedrooms.
- Elegant main floor master bedroom enjoys privacy, special window and tiered ceiling.
- Pampering bath/dressing area features whirlpool, his and her vanities and large walk-in closet.

First Floor	1,509 sq. ft.
Second Floor	661 sq. ft.
Total Living Area	2,170 sq. ft.

PRICE CODE: C

CUSTOMIZE IT!

ORDER TOLL FREE   1■800■533■4350   24-HOUR FAX ORDERING   1■800■344■4293

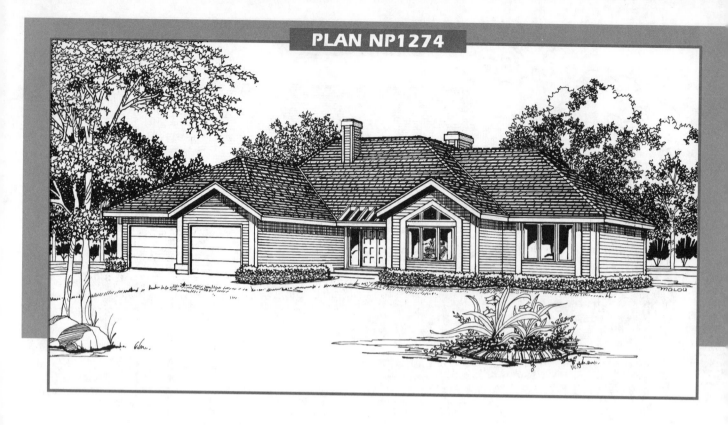

106

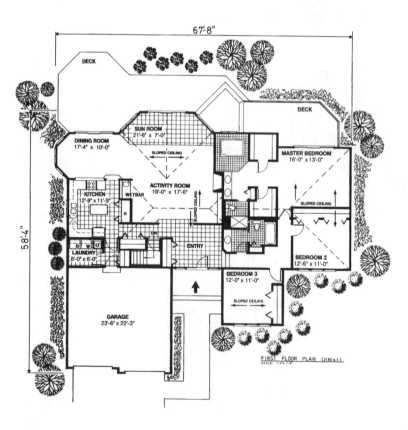

67'-8"

DECK

SUN ROOM
21'-6" x 7'-0"

DECK

DINING ROOM
17'-4" x 10'-0"

SLOPED CEILING

MASTER BEDROOM
16'-0" x 13'-0"

58'-4"

KITCHEN
12'-9" x 11'-9"

WETBAR

ACTIVITY ROOM
19'-0" x 17'-6"

SLOPED CEILING

SLOPED CEILING

LAUNDRY
8'-0" x 6'-0"

ENTRY

BEDROOM 2
12'-6" x 11'-0"

BEDROOM 3
12'-0" x 11'-0"

GARAGE
23'-6" x 22'-3"

SLOPED CEILING

FIRST FLOOR PLAN (2180 s.f.)
SCALE: 1/2" = 1'-0"

Total Living Area   **2,180 sq. ft.**

PRICE CODE: B

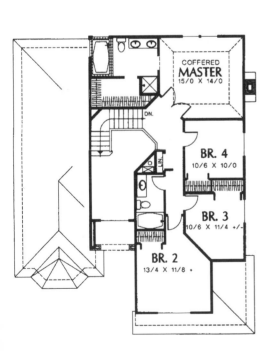

Second Floor:
- COFFERED MASTER 15/0 X 14/0
- BR. 4 10/6 X 10/0
- BR. 3 10/6 X 11/4 +/-
- BR. 2 13/4 X 11/8 +

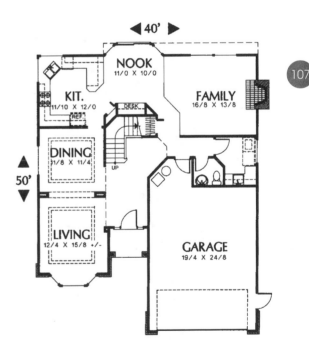

First Floor:
- NOOK 11/0 X 10/0
- KIT. 11/10 X 12/0
- FAMILY 16/8 X 13/8
- DINING 11/8 X 11/4
- DESK
- LIVING 12/4 X 15/8 +/-
- GARAGE 19/4 X 24/8

◀ 40' ▶

▲ 50' ▼

107

First Floor	1,166 sq. ft.
Second Floor	1,019 sq. ft.
Total Living Area	2,185 sq. ft.

PRICE CODE: B

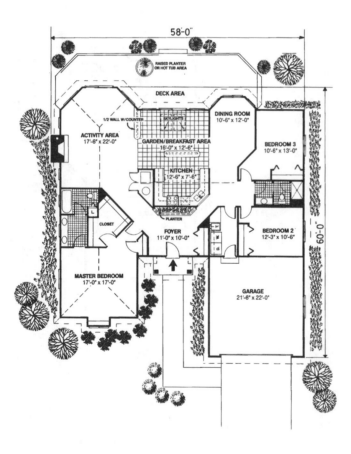

Great Expectations

Features

- Comfort and good-looks are combined in this design for modern families.
- Perfect for those who love a sense of indoor/outdoor living.
- Enter pillared main entrance to the foyer with built-in planter.
- Right wing includes two bedrooms with full bath and laundry room with access to garage.
- Left wing features the enormous master bedroom with private bath and compartmented shower and water closet plus a cozy window seat.
- Rear of home features centrally located kitchen and garden/breakfast area with access to optional rear deck with raised planter or optional hot tub.

Total Living Area   **2,190 sq. ft.**

PRICE CODE: B

PLAN JA5399

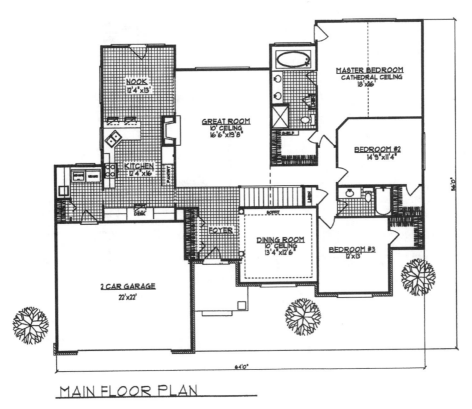

MASTER BEDROOM
CATHEDRAL CEILING
18'x16'

NOOK
12'4"x13'

GREAT ROOM
10' CEILING
16'6"x19'8"

BEDROOM #2
14'9"x11'4"

KITCHEN
12'4"x16'

FOYER

DINING ROOM
10' CEILING
13'4"x12'6"

BEDROOM #3
12'x13'

2 CAR GARAGE
22'x22'

64'0"

56'0"

MAIN FLOOR PLAN

Total Living Area   2,204 sq. ft.

PRICE CODE: C

CUSTOMIZE IT!

ORDER TOLL FREE   1 ▪ 800 ▪ 533 ▪ 4350   24-HOUR FAX ORDERING   1 ▪ 800 ▪ 344 ▪ 4293

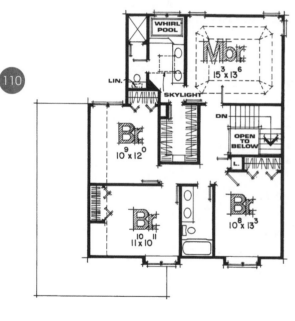

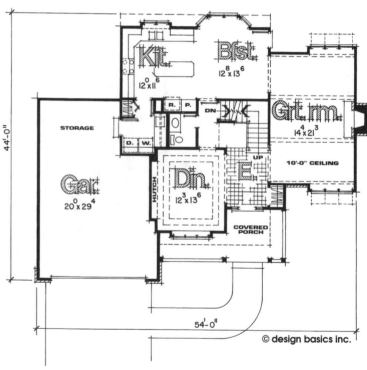

© design basics inc.

Features

- Open central core at staircase.
- 10-foot ceiling in great room with fireplace as focal point.
- Large, beautiful boxed windows at front and back of great room.
- Formal, tiered ceiling in dining room.
- Large island kitchen and dinette.
- Laundry room with coat closet serves as mud entry from garage.
- Additional storage space in garage.
- Secondary bedrooms share central bath with double vanity.
- Master bedroom at top of stairs buffered from secondary bedrooms.
- Master bath area includes double lav vanity, whirlpool tub, large walk-in closet and skylight.

First Floor   1,132 sq. ft.
Second Floor   1,087 sq. ft.
Total Living Area   2,219 sq. ft.

PRICE CODE: D

CUSTOMIZE IT!

ORDER TOLL FREE   1 ■ 800 ■ 533 ■ 4350   24-HOUR FAX ORDERING   1 ■ 800 ■ 344 ■ 4293

PLAN DB2176

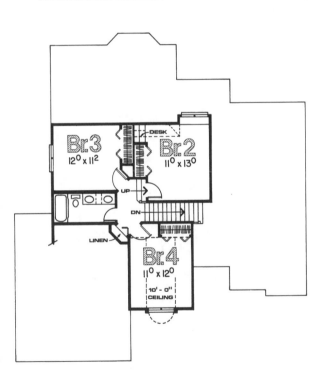

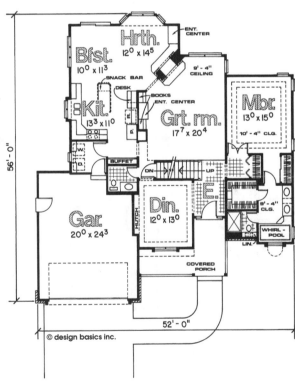

111

© design basics inc.

Features

- Generous covered front porch.
- Great room features bookcases, entertainment center and angled see-thru fireplace.
- Island kitchen offers abundant amenities including built-in buffet serving counter for formal dining convenience.
- Hearth room with bayed window and entertainment center.
- Convenient utility entrance.

- Double doors into master bedroom with tiered ceiling
- Master dressing area with whirlpool under arched window.
- Upstairs, bedroom #4 has beautiful arched window with volume ceiling.

First Floor	**1,595 sq. ft.**
Second Floor	**641 sq. ft.**
Total Living Area	**2,236 sq. ft.**

PRICE CODE: D

CUSTOMIZE IT!

ORDER TOLL FREE **1 ▪ 800 ▪ 533 ▪ 4350** 24-HOUR FAX ORDERING **1 ▪ 800 ▪ 344 ▪ 4293**

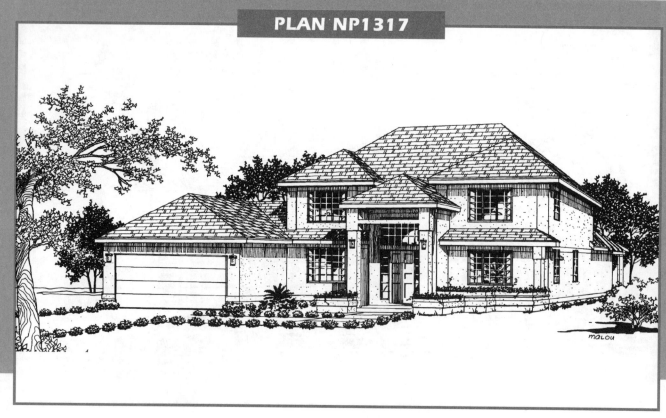

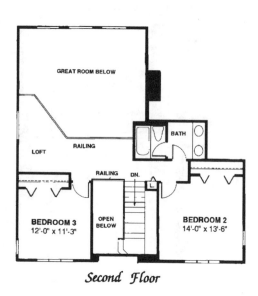

Second Floor

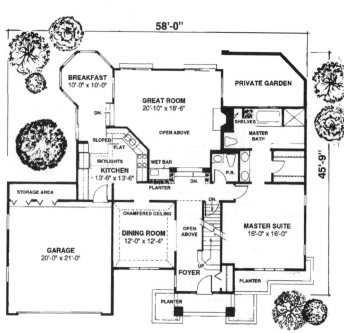

First Floor
Plan 1 with Basement

Sunny Stucco

Features

- Impressive stucco exterior and large windows makes this home a sun-worshippers haven.
- Front entrance features built-in planters on either side.
- Large open foyer is open above.
- Formal dining room has beautiful chamfered ceiling.

- Hall to kitchen includes built-in planter.
- Kitchen incorporates skylights and octagonal breakfast nook.
- First-floor master suite of impressive dimensions.
- Second-floor loft overlooks great room.

First Floor	1,599 sq. ft.
Second Floor	725 sq. ft.
Total Living Area	2,324 sq. ft.

PRICE CODE: C

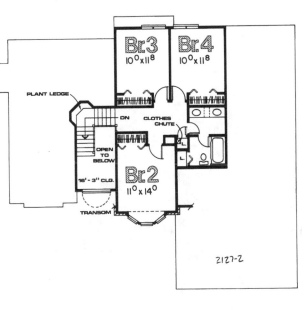

2127-2

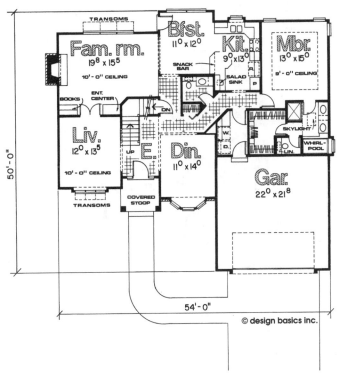

113

© design basics inc.

Features

- Beautiful bayed window in dining room.
- French doors between living room and family room for versatility.
- Handsome fireplace, entertainment center, bookcase and windows are all a part of the family room.
- Boxed ceiling in private master bedroom.

- Skylit master dressing/bath area with decorate or plant ledge above, double vanity and whirlpool under window.
- Angled landing on stairs.
- Bayed window for bedroom #2.
- Second level bedrooms share compartmented hall bath with 2 lavs.

First Floor	**1,602 sq. ft.**
Second Floor	**654 sq. ft.**
Total Living Area	**2,256 sq. ft.**

PRICE CODE: D

CUSTOMIZE IT!

ORDER TOLL FREE 1■800■533■4350   **24-HOUR FAX ORDERING** 1■800■344■4293

114

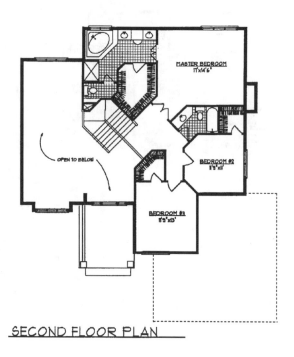

SECOND FLOOR PLAN

MAIN FLOOR PLAN

First Floor	1,271 sq. ft.
Second Floor	991 sq. ft.
Total Living Area	2,262 sq. ft.

PRICE CODE: C

PLAN DB1554

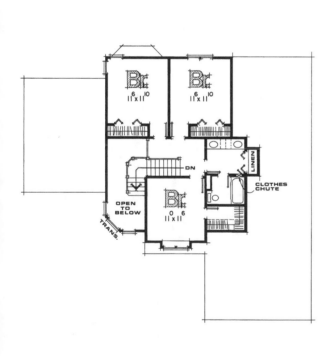

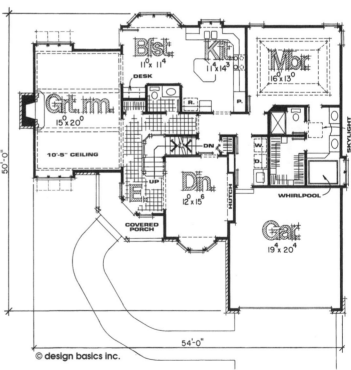

115

Features

- Wrapping porch at entry.
- 2-story-high entry open to formal dining room with beautiful bayed windows
- Handsome fireplace and 10 1/2-foot ceiling in great room.
- Well-equipped island kitchen with pantry and built-in desk for the serious cook.

- Large master bedroom with vaulted ceiling.
- Luxury master bath with 2-person whirlpool, skylight and large walk-in closet.
- Stairs leading to corridor hall.
- Generous secondary bedrooms with ample closet space.

First Floor	1,551 sq. ft.
Second Floor	725 sq. ft.
Total Living Area	2,276 sq. ft.

PRICE CODE: D

CUSTOMIZE IT!

ORDER TOLL FREE 1 ■ 800 ■ 533 ■ 4350   *24-HOUR FAX ORDERING*   1 ■ 800 ■ 344 ■ 4293

PLAN AM2258D

116

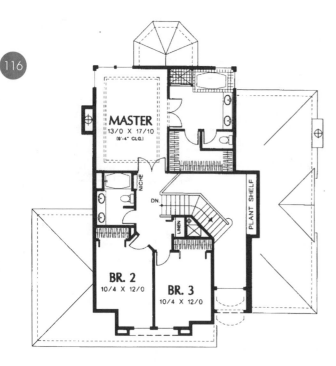

MASTER
13/0 X 17/10
(9'-4" CLG.)

NICHE

DN.

PLANT SHELF

LINEN

BR. 2
10/4 X 12/0

BR. 3
10/4 X 12/0

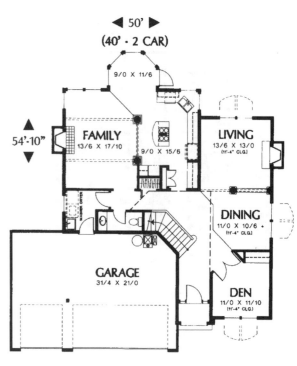

◄ 50' ►
(40' - 2 CAR)

9/0 X 11/6

54'-10"

FAMILY
13/6 X 17/10

9/0 X 15/6

LIVING
13/6 X 13/0
(11'-4" CLG.)

DINING
11/0 X 10/6 +
(11'-4" CLG.)

GARAGE
31/4 X 21/0

DEN
11/0 X 11/10
(11'-4" CLG.)

First Floor	1,322 sq. ft.
Second Floor	1,000 sq. ft.
Total Living Area	2,322 sq. ft.

PRICE CODE: C

PLAN SH1188-2268

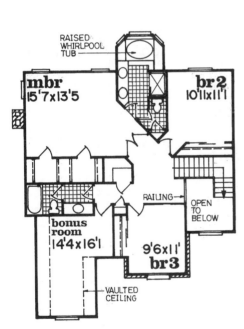

RAISED WHIRLPOOL TUB

mbr 15'7x13'5

br2 10'11x11'1

RAILING

OPEN TO BELOW

bonus room 14'4x16'1

br3 9'6x11'

VAULTED CEILING

SECOND LEVEL 966 sq. ft.

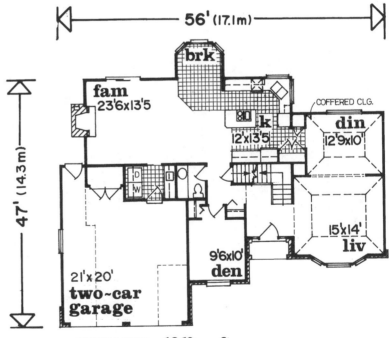

56' (17.1m)

117

47' (14.3 m)

brk

fam 23'6x13'5

COFFERED CLG.

k 12'x13'5

din 12'9x10'

21'x20' two-car garage

9'6x10' den

15'x14' **liv**

FIRST LEVEL 1360 sq. ft.

Features

- Brick detailing and dominant arched windows adorn this home.
- Living and dining rooms boast coffered ceilings.
- Centre cooking island adds efficiency to the open plan kitchen.
- Breakfast bay extends to the large family room.

- Vaulted foyer with circle-top window ascends to a railed gallery.
- Ensuite has a whirlpool tucked in a bay window.
- Bonus room provides an additional 198 square feet of living space.

Total Living Area   2,326 sq. ft.

PRICE CODE: C

CUSTOMIZE IT!

ORDER TOLL FREE **1▪800▪533▪4350**   24-HOUR FAX ORDERING **1▪800▪344▪4293**

◀ 60' ▶

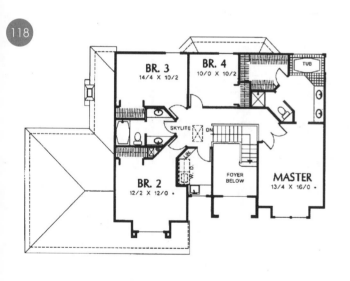

BR. 3
14/4 X 10/2

BR. 4
10/0 X 10/2

TUB

SKYLITE   DN

BR. 2
12/2 X 12/0

FOYER
BELOW

MASTER
13/4 X 16/0

▲
40'
▼

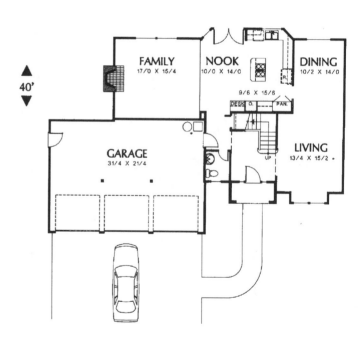

FAMILY
17/0 X 15/4

NOOK
10/0 X 14/0

DINING
10/2 X 14/0

9/6 X 15/6

DESK   PAN.

GARAGE
31/4 X 21/4

LIVING
13/4 X 15/2

UP

First Floor	1,172 sq. ft.
Second Floor	1,214 sq. ft.
Total Living Area	2,386 sq. ft.

PRICE CODE: C

119

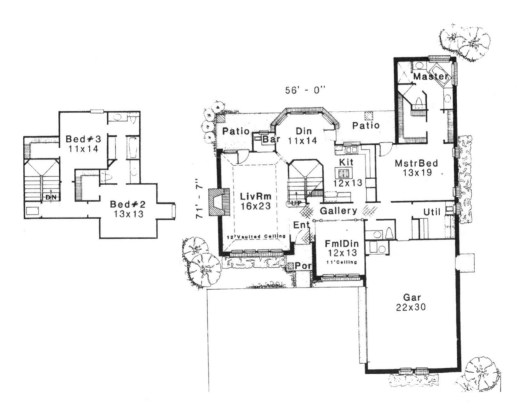

56' - 0"

71' - 7"

Bed#3
11x14

Bed#2
13x13

DN

Patio

Bar

Din
11x14

Patio

Master

Kit
12x13

MstrBed
13x19

LivRm
16x23

UP

Gallery

Util

Ent

12'Vaulted Ceiling

FmlDin
12x13
11'Ceiling

Por

Gar
22x30

First Floor	1,755 sq. ft.
Second Floor	647 sq. ft.
Total Living Area	2,402 sq. ft.

PRICE CODE: C

CUSTOMIZE IT!

ORDER TOLL FREE   1■800■533■4350   **24-HOUR FAX ORDERING**   1■800■344■4293

PLAN AM2244A

120

◄ 58' ►

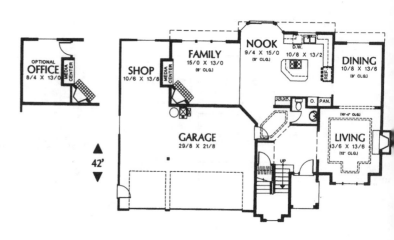

42'

First Floor	1,216 sq. ft.
Second Floor	1,192 sq. ft.
Total Living Area	2,408 sq. ft.
Office	+140 sq. ft.

PRICE CODE: C

PLAN FD7756A

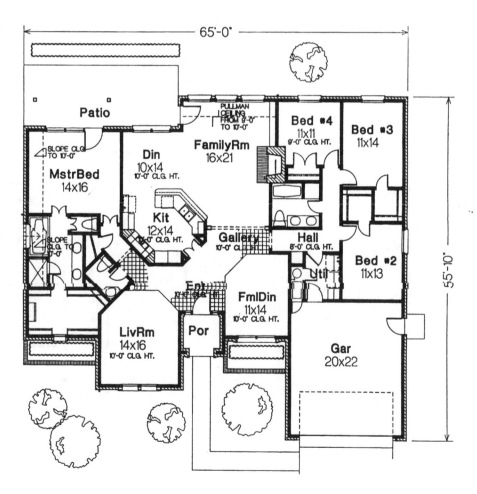

Patio

Din
10x14
10'-0" CLG. HT.

MstrBed
14x16

SLOPE CLG
TO 10'-0"

SLOPE CLG
TO 10'-0"

PULLMAN
CEILING
FROM 9'-0"
TO 10'-0"

FamilyRm
16x21

Bed #4
11x11
9'-0" CLG. HT.

Bed #3
11x14

Kit
12x14
10'-0" CLG. HT.

Gallery
10'-0" CLG. HT.

Hall
8'-0" CLG. HT.

Bed #2
11x13

Ent

Util

FmlDin
11x14
10'-0" CLG. HT.

LivRm
14x16
10'-0" CLG. HT.

Por

Gar
20x22

65'-0"

55'-10"

121

Total Living Area   2,425 sq. ft.

PRICE CODE: C

CUSTOMIZE IT!

ORDER TOLL FREE   1■800■533■4350   24-HOUR FAX ORDERING   1■800■344■4293

122

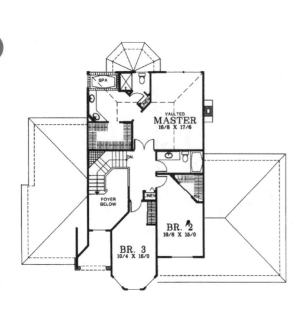

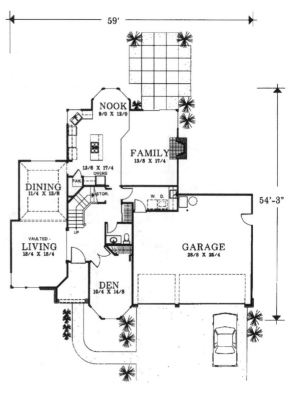

First Floor	1,408 sq. ft
Second Floor	1,024 sq. ft
Total Living Area	2,432 sq. ft

PRICE CODE: C

Total Living Area   **2,439 sq. ft.**

PRICE CODE: C

◀ 53' ▶

124

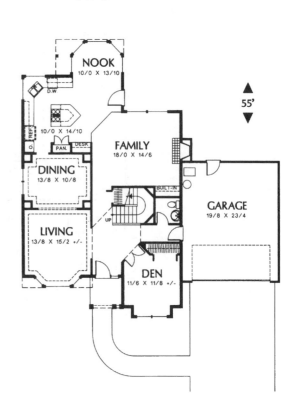

55'

First Floor	1,409 sq. ft.
Second Floor	1,034 sq. ft.
Total Living Area	2,443 sq. ft.

PRICE CODE: C

PLAN AM2228L

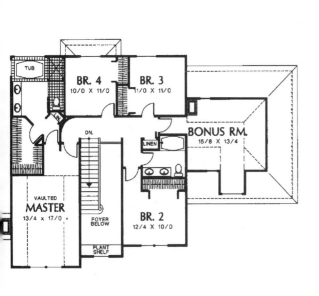

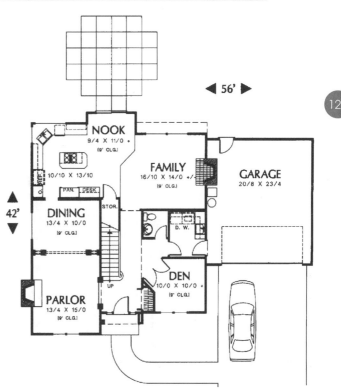

125

◀ 56' ▶

First Floor   1,308 sq. ft.
Second Floor   1,141 sq. ft.
Total Living Area   2,449 sq. ft.
Bonus Room   +266 sq. ft.

PRICE CODE: C

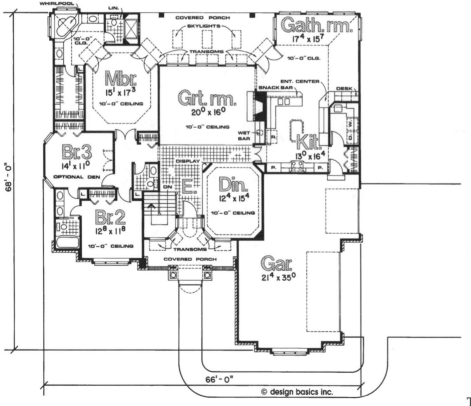

WHIRLPOOL

LIN.

COVERED PORCH

SKYLIGHTS

Gath. rm.
17⁴ x 15⁷

10'-0" CLG.

TRANSOMS

Mbr.
15¹ x 17³
10'-0" CEILING

10'-0" CLG.

ENT. CENTER

SNACK BAR

DESK

Grt. rm.
20⁰ x 16⁰
10'-0" CEILING

WET BAR

Kit.
13⁰ x 16⁴

Br. 3
14¹ x 11⁰

OPTIONAL DEN

DISPLAY

DN

Din.
12⁴ x 15⁴
10'-0" CEILING

P.

P.

Br. 2
12⁸ x 11⁸

10'-0" CEILING

TRANSOMS

COVERED PORCH

Gar.
21⁴ x 35⁰

68' - 0"

66' - 0"

© design basics inc.

Features

- Tapered columns at entry create majestic front elevation.
- Open great room features wet bar, fireplace and tall windows allowing natural light.
- Wide kitchen features ideally placed island, 2 pantries and easy laundry access.
- Double doors open to master suite with French doors leading to master bath and covered porch.
- Enjoy beauty and convenience of master bath with whirlpool, dual lavs, plant shelves and large walk-in closet.

Total Living Area   2,456 sq

PRICE CODE: D

CUSTOMIZE IT!

ORDER TOLL FREE 1■800■533■4350   24-HOUR FAX ORDERING 1■800■344■4293

127

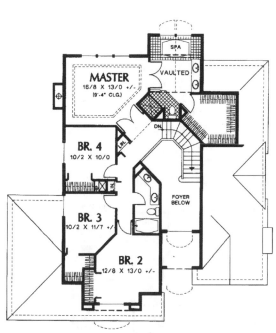

MASTER
16/8 X 13/0 +/-
(9'-4" CLG.)

SPA

VAULTED

BR. 4
10/2 X 10/0

DN.

FOYER
BELOW

BR. 3
10/2 X 11/7 +/-

BR. 2
12/8 X 13/0 +/-

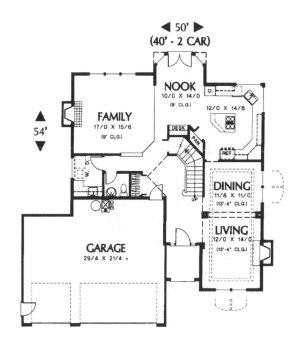

◄ 50' ►
(40' - 2 CAR)

NOOK
10/0 X 14/0
(9' CLG.)

12/0 X 14/8

FAMILY
17/0 X 15/6
(9' CLG.)

▲
54'
▼

DESK

PAN.

REF.

W. D.

UP

DINING
11/8 X 11/0
(13'-4" CLG.)

GARAGE
29/4 X 21/4 +

LIVING
12/0 X 14/0
(13'-4" CLG.)

First Floor	1,317 sq. ft.
Second Floor	1,146 sq. ft.
Total Living Area	2,463 sq. ft.

PRICE CODE: C

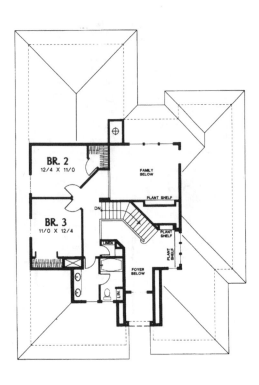

BR. 2
12/4 X 11/0

FAMILY
BELOW

PLANT SHELF

BR. 3
11/0 X 12/4

DN

PLANT
SHELF

PLANT
SHELF

LINEN

FOYER
BELOW

LIN.

◀ 45' ▶

MASTER
13/0 X 16/0
(10' CLG.)

SPA

DEN
11/0 X 10/0
(9' CLG.)

MEDIA CENTER

LINEN

NOOK
11/4 x 10/0
(9' CLG.)

TWO STORY
FAMILY
17/4 X 16/8 +/-

11/0 X 11/4 +/-

(9' CLG.)

BUILT-IN

W   D

REF.

64'

▲
▼

UP

DINING
12/0 x 10/10
(10' CLG.)

GARAGE
20/4 X 21/8

LIVING
13/0 x 14/6
(10' CLG.)

First Floor	1,896 sq. ft
Second Floor	568 sq. ft
Total Living Area	2,464 sq. ft

PLAN AM2211C

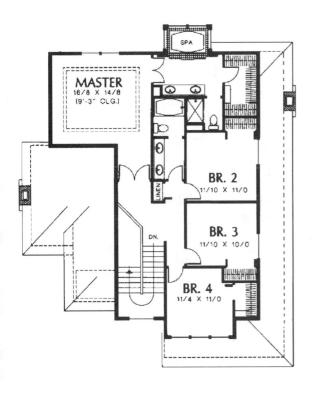

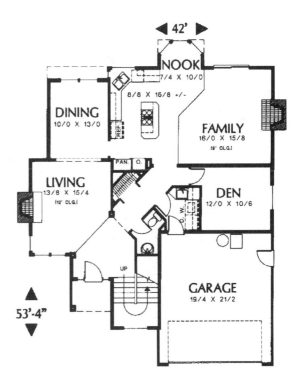

First Floor	1,321 sq. ft.
Second Floor	1,155 sq. ft.
Total Living Area	2,476 sq. ft.

PRICE CODE: C

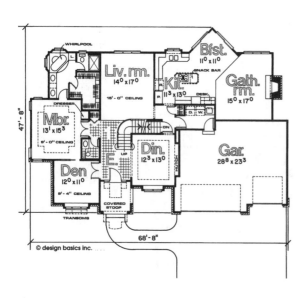

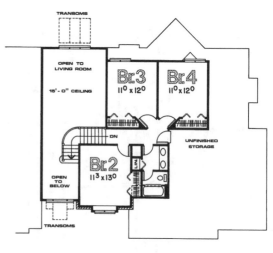

Features

- Impactful front elevation with elegant window and trim details.
- Impressive entry views formal dining room, den with French doors and volume living room with transoms.
- Attractive design of gourmet kitchen, breakfast area and gathering room gives a peaceful retreat.
- Secondary bedrooms on second level share compartmented bath.

- Luxurious master suite offers seclusion and includes pocket door to front den for ready use as a home office or retreat.
- Elegant compartmented master bath and dressing area includes corner whirlpool and huge walk-in closet.

First Floor	1,829 sq. ft.
Second Floor	657 sq. ft.
Total Living Area	2,486 sq. ft.

PRICE CODE: D

◀ 50' ▶
(40' - 2 CAR)

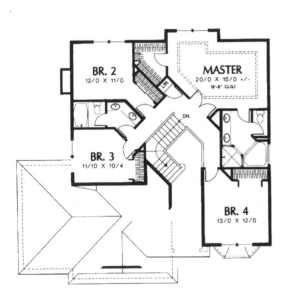

BR. 2
12/0 X 11/0

MASTER
20/0 X 15/0 +/-
(9'-6" CLG.)

LIN.

DN.

BR. 3
11/10 X 10/4

BR. 4
13/0 X 12/0

▲
48'
▼

FAMILY RM.
18/4 X 14/6
(9' CLG.)

NOOK
11/0 X 15/8

10/0 X 16/0

DINING
13/0 X 11/0

UP

GARAGE
19/4 X 21/0

10/0 X 19/4

LIVING
13/0 X 13/8 +/-

First Floor	1,304 sq. ft.
Second Floor	1,190 sq. ft.
Total Living Area	2,494 sq. ft.

PRICE CODE: C

CUSTOMIZE IT!

ORDER TOLL FREE   1■800■533■4350   24-HOUR FAX ORDERING   1■800■344■4293

PLAN FD7056-LB

Pool

FamilyRm
16x17

Patio

70' - 0''

Cathedral Ceiling

Bar

MstrBed
14x17
9'Ceiling

Master

Din
12x12
9'Ceiling

9'Ceiling

LivRm
15x17
10'Ceiling

Kit
10x15

Bed #4
11x12

Gallery

Ent

73' - 4''

Bed#3
11x11

B #3

Util

Dining
11x12
10'Ceiling

B #2

Bed #2
11x13

Por

Gar
22x22

Total Living Area   2,495 sq. ft.

SECOND FLOOR

FIRST FLOOR
PLAN 2 WITHOUT BASEMENT

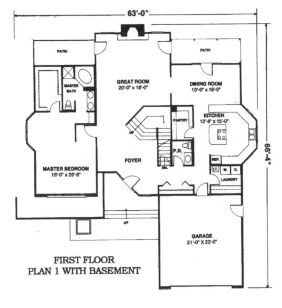

FIRST FLOOR
PLAN 1 WITH BASEMENT

Monmouth

Features

- Appearances can be deceiving -- this home looks enormous but boasts more modest dimensions inside, without sacrificing comfort.
- Columnar entrance leads into spacious foyer with dramatic, platform stairs.
- Left wing includes master bedroom suite, with dual-vanity master bath, walk-in closet, and raised Roman tub.
- Large great room with fireplace and patio access occupies the rear of the home.
- Bayed kitchen with cooking island adjoins dining room, also with patio access.
- Upstairs are two additional bedrooms that share a full bath.

First Floor	**1,854 sq. ft.**
Second Floor	**652 sq. ft.**
Total Living Area	**2,506 sq. ft.**

PRICE CODE: C

CUSTOMIZE IT!

ORDER TOLL FREE 1∎800∎533∎4350   24-HOUR FAX ORDERING 1∎800∎344∎4293

134

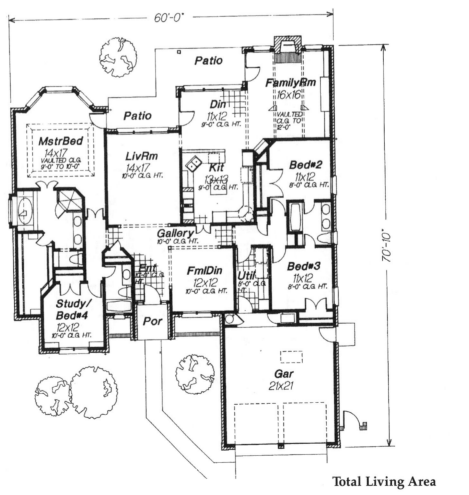

Total Living Area   **2,506 sq. ft.**

PRICE CODE: C

PLAN AM2227B

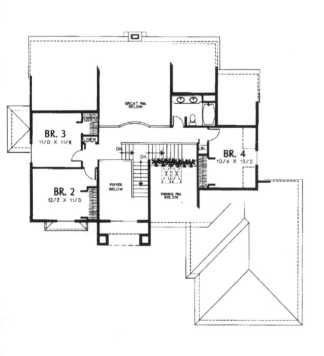

First Floor	1,784 sq. ft.
Second Floor	742 sq. ft.
Total Living Area	2,526 sq. ft.

PRICE CODE: C

CUSTOMIZE IT!

ORDER TOLL FREE   **1▪800▪533▪4350**   **24-HOUR FAX ORDERING**   **1▪800▪344▪4293**

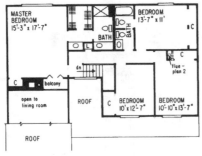

SECOND FLOOR

Herringbone Manor

Features

- Varied roof lines and herringbone siding patterns give this contemporary home a dramatic flair.
- Sunken living room with sloped ceiling and a fireplace that serves both the living room and family room.
- U-shaped kitchen with adjacent breakfast area at rear of home with view of back yard.
- Second floor master bedroom has a large, walk-in closet, full bath with double vanity, and balcony overlooking the living room.
- Three additional bedrooms share a large bath.

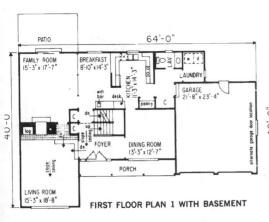

FIRST FLOOR PLAN 1 WITH BASEMENT

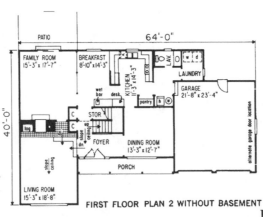

FIRST FLOOR PLAN 2 WITHOUT BASEMENT

First Floor	1,368 sq. ft
Second Floor	1,160 sq. ft
Total Living Area	2,528 sq. ft

PRICE CODE: C

PLAN MN2537

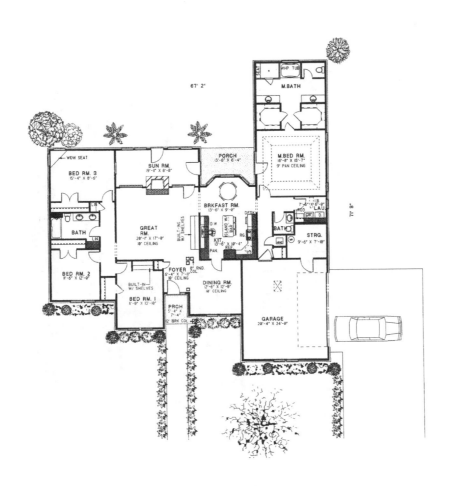

Total Living Area   2,537 sq. ft.

PRICE CODE: C

CUSTOMIZE IT!

ORDER TOLL FREE   **1 ▪ 800 ▪ 533 ▪ 4350**   24-HOUR FAX ORDERING   **1 ▪ 800 ▪ 344 ▪ 4293**

PLAN FD7126-L

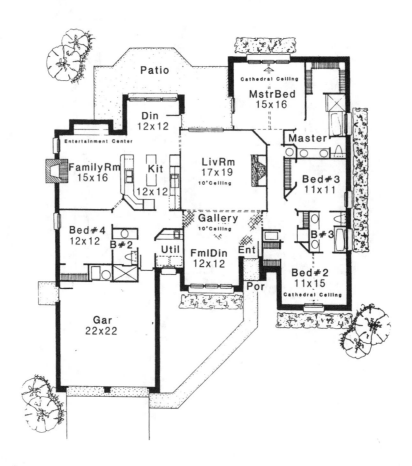

138

Patio

Din 12x12

MstrBed 15x16
Cathedral Ceiling

Entertainment Center

FamilyRm 15x16

Kit 12x12

LivRm 17x19
10'Ceiling

Master

Bed #3 11x11

Bed #4 12x12

B#2

Util

Gallery 10'Ceiling

FmlDin 12x12

Ent

B#3

Por

Bed #2 11x15
Cathedral Ceiling

Gar 22x22

Total Living Area   2,547 sq. ft.

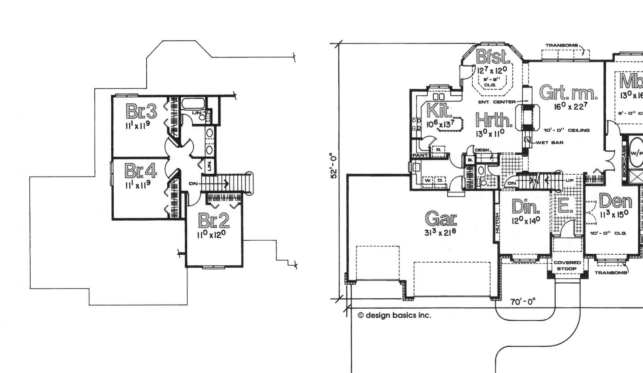

139

© design basics inc.

Features

- Stone and stucco coupled with excellent lines add intriguing curb appeal.
- Splendid entry hall surveys formal dining and great rooms with special amenities.
- Kitchen/breakfast/hearth room features corner walk-in pantry and built-in desk.
- Great room's see-thru fireplace flanked by pass-thru wet bar/servery and entertainment center.

- Secondary bedrooms secluded on second level include large closets and share compartmented bath with dual lavs.
- French door entry to hall with built-in bookcases between master suite and private den.
- Exquisite master bath/dressing area with his and her lavs, oval whirlpool and spacious walk-in closet.

First Floor	1,933 sq. ft.
Second Floor	646 sq. ft.
Total Living Area	2,579 sq. ft.

PRICE CODE: D

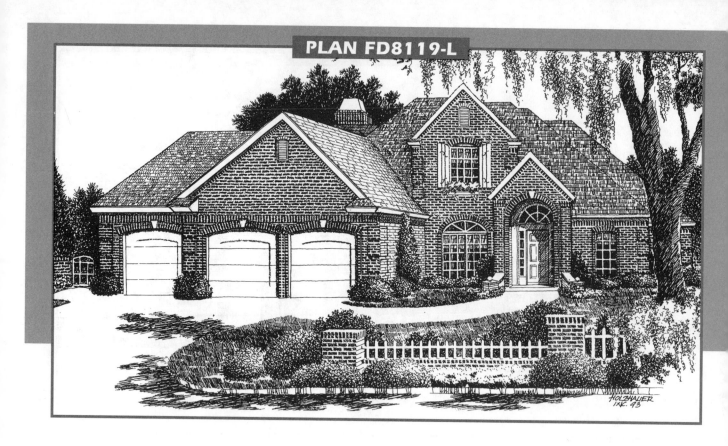

140

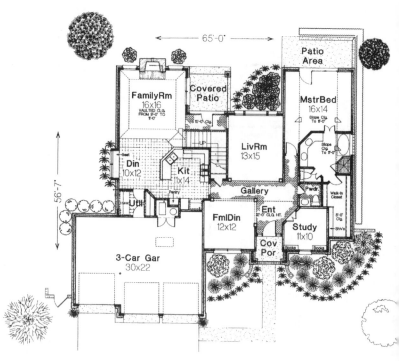

First Floor	1,871 sq. ft.
Second Floor	727 sq. ft.
Total Living Area	2,598 sq. ft.

PRICE CODE: C

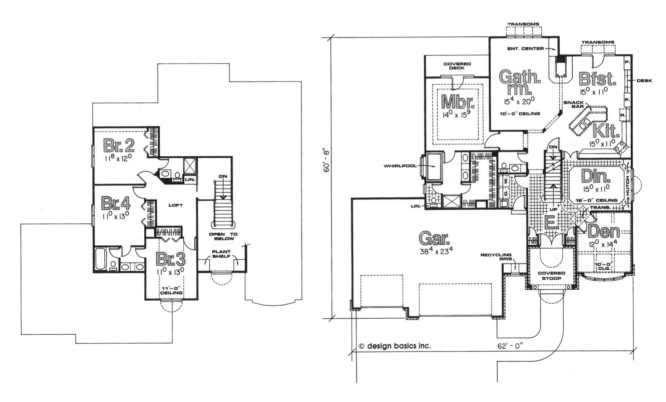

141

Features

- Columns and double doors at entry create a majestic elevation.
- 12-foot-tall dining room open to spacious 2-story entry.
- Spider beams and bowed window add sophistication to den.
- French doors in dining room open to island kitchen and dinette which share 3-sided fireplace

with gathering room.
- Secluded master suite boasts private covered deck, whirlpool bath and large walk-in closet.
- Popular 3-car garage includes recycling center and convenient laundry room access.
- Bedroom #2 has private 3/4 bath and a compartmented bath has private access from bedrooms #3 and #4.

First Floor	1,800 sq. ft.
Second Floor	803 sq. ft.
Total Living Area	2,603 sq. ft.

PRICE CODE: D

CUSTOMIZE IT!

ORDER TOLL FREE 1 ▪ 800 ▪ 533 ▪ 4350   24-HOUR FAX ORDERING   1 ▪ 800 ▪ 344 ▪ 4293

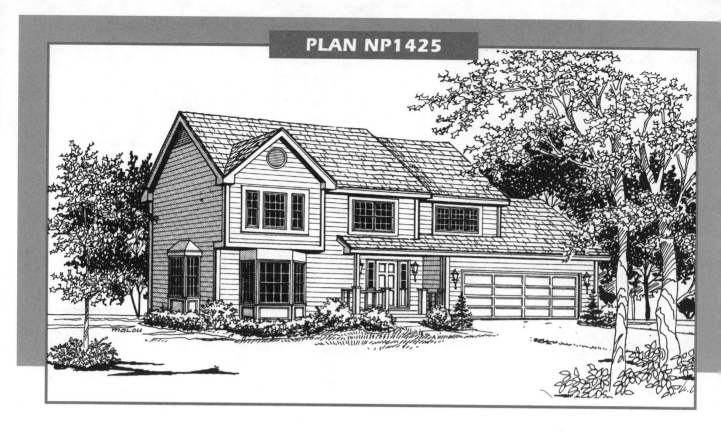

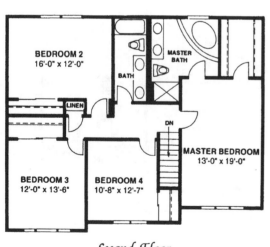

Second Floor

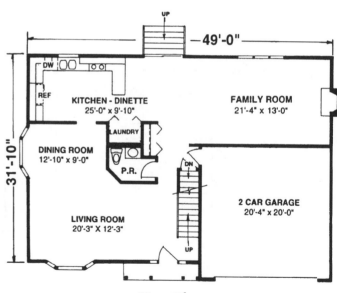

First Floor

Sunnyview

Features

- Handsome two-story design perfect for the growing family.
- Attractive porch entrance opens directly into a large family room with adjoining dining room.
- Dining room features an elegant bay window.
- Large family room with fireplace perfect for family activities.

- Upstairs, a large master bedroom with spacious walk-in closet and deluxe, dual- vanity bath with step-up tub and separate shower.
- Three additional spacious bedrooms share a full bath with dual-vanity.

First Floor	1,192 sq. ft.
Second Floor	1,425 sq. ft.
Total Living Area	2,617 sq. ft.

PRICE CODE: C

CUSTOMIZE IT!

ORDER TOLL FREE 1 ▪ 800 ▪ 533 ▪ 4350   **24-HOUR FAX ORDERING** 1 ▪ 800 ▪ 344 ▪ 4293

PLAN SH91-2538

143

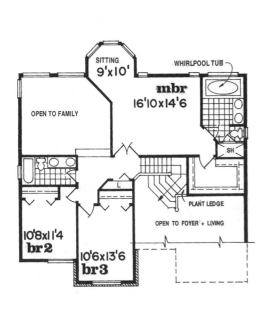

second level
1154 sq.ft.

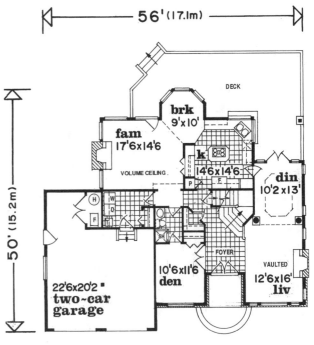

first level
1464 sq.ft.

Features

- High vaulted ceilings and floor to ceiling window enhance the spaciousness throughout the foyer and living room.
- Decorative columns visually separate the living room from the trayed ceiling dining room; French doors beyond open to the expansive rear deck.
- Gourmet kitchen offers a centre preparation island, pantry pass-through to the family room, and breakfast bay.
- Spacious family room with fireplace boasts a vaulted ceiling which is open to the second-level hallway.
- Master bedroom features a bay window sitting area, walk-in closet and ensuite with whirlpool spa, twin vanity and plan shower.

First Floor	1,464 sq. ft.
Second Floor	1,154 sq. ft.
Total Living Area	2,618 sq. ft.

PRICE CODE: C

C U S T O M I Z E   I T !

ORDER TOLL FREE 1■800■533■4350   **24-HOUR FAX ORDERING** 1■800■344■4293

144

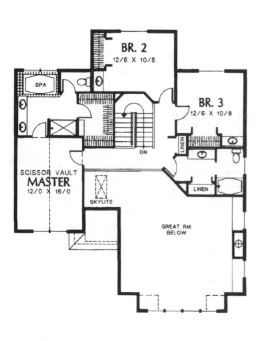

BR. 2
12/6 X 10/8

SPA

BR. 3
12/6 X 10/8

LINEN

LINEN

DN

SCISSOR VAULT
MASTER
12/0 X 16/0

SKYLITE

GREAT RM.
BELOW

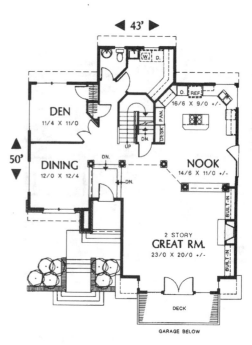

◀ 43' ▶

W D

REF

DESK PAN

DEN
11/4 X 11/0

16/6 X 9/0 +/-

50'

UP   DN.

DINING
12/0 X 12/4

DN.

DN.

NOOK
14/6 X 11/0 +/-

BUILT-IN

BUILT-IN

2 STORY
GREAT RM.
23/0 X 20/0 +/-

DECK

GARAGE BELOW

First Floor	1,538 sq. ft.
Second Floor	1,089 sq. ft.
Total Living Area	2,627 sq. ft.

PRICE CODE: C

Total Living Area   2,626 sq. ft.

PRICE CODE: C

CUSTOMIZE IT!

ORDER TOLL FREE   1■800■533■4350   24-HOUR FAX ORDERING   1■800■344■4293

PLAN FD8037-LB

65'-0"

66'-10"

Patio Area

Din 8x10
9'-0" Clg

FamilyRm 16x15
9'-0" Clg

MstrBed 15x17
Vaulted Clg From 8'-0" To 11'-0"

Study 12x12
10'-0" Clg

Kit 14x12

Bed#2 12x11

Walk-In Closet

Sloped Clg From 8'-0" To 10'-0"

Gallery
9'-0" Clg

Bed#4 12x10

Linen

Ent
9'-0" Clg

FmlDin 12x12
9'-0" Clg

Util.

Bed#3 12x11

LivRm 14x15
10'-0" Clg

Cov. Por.

Gar 22x23
8'-4" Clg

Total Living Area   2,626 sq. ft.

CUSTOMIZE IT!

ORDER TOLL FREE   1■800■533■4350   24-HOUR FAX ORDERING   1■800■344■4293

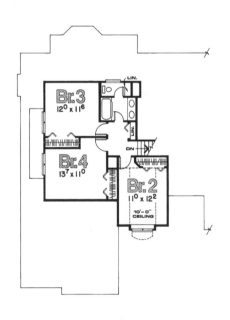

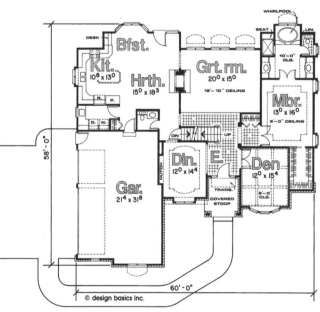

Features

- Elevation incorporates rhythmic use of gables and arches plus stucco accents for instant curb appeal.
- Dining room has decorative boxed ceiling and space to accommodate buffet or hutch.
- Versatile den has double-door entrance and classic spider-beamed ceiling.
- Kitchen designed for efficiency and convenience with 2 lazy Susan, pantry, food preparation island .

- See-thru fireplace between volume great room and open hearth room.
- French doors access handsome master bedroom.
- Pampering dressing room features large whirlpool, shower and dual lavs.

First Floor	1,972 sq. ft.
Second Floor	673 sq. ft.
Total Living Area	2,645 sq. ft.

PRICE CODE: D

CUSTOMIZE IT!

ORDER TOLL FREE 1 ■ 800 ■ 533 ■ 4350   **24-HOUR FAX ORDERING** 1 ■ 800 ■ 344 ■ 4293

148

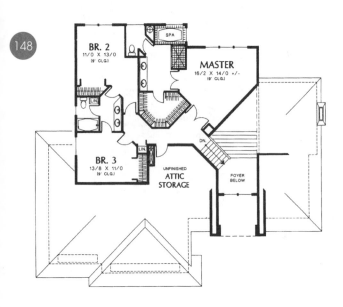

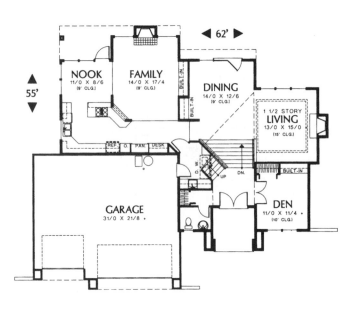

PLAN IS DESIGNED FOR LOTS THAT SLOPE TO
THE NEAR AND TO THE LEFT SIDE

First Floor	**1,532 sq. ft.**
Second Floor	**1,116 sq. ft.**
Total Living Area	**2,648 sq. ft.**

PRICE CODE: C

PLAN DB1810

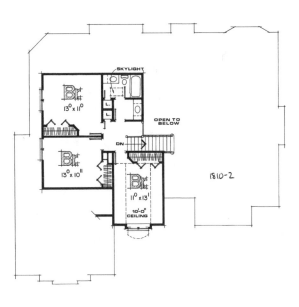

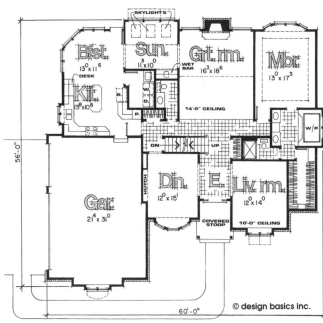

149

Features

- Hutch space and bayed windows in dining room.
- Central hall entry leads to volume great room with fireplace.
- Volume sun room with triple skylights and wet bar.
- Deluxe island kitchen with pantry and planning desk adjoins angled dinette.

- Luxury whirlpool bath with 2 lavs, make-up counter and large walk-in closet.
- Stairs lead to corridor hallway accessing secondary bedrooms.
- Secondary bedrooms share skylit compartmented bath.
- 3-car side-load garage.

First Floor	**1,941 sq. ft.**
Second Floor	**722 sq. ft.**
Total Living Area	**2,663 sq. ft.**

PRICE CODE: D

CUSTOMIZE IT!

ORDER TOLL FREE 1■800■533■4350 **24-HOUR FAX ORDERING** 1■800■344■4293

PLAN SH1188-2453

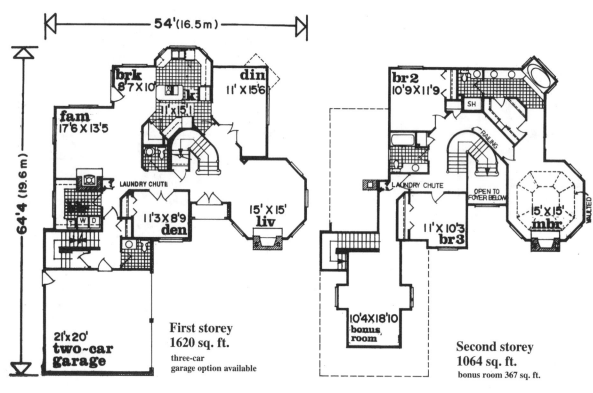

54' (16.5m)

64'4" (19.6 m)

brk 8'7 X 10

din 11' X 15'6

fam 17'6 X 13'5

k 11' X 15'

LAUNDRY CHUTE

11'3 X 8'9 **den**

15' X 15' **liv**

W D

21' X 20' **two-car garage**

First storey 1620 sq. ft.

three-car garage option available

br2 10'9 X 11'9

SH

RAILING

LAUNDRY CHUTE

OPEN TO FOYER BELOW

5' X 15' **mbr** VAULTED

11' X 10'3 **br3**

10'4 X 18'10 **bonus room**

Second storey 1064 sq. ft.

bonus room 367 sq. ft.

Features

- Sweeping, horseshoe-shaped staircase dominates the two-storey foyer.
- Octagonal living room has a masonry fireplace.
- Kitchen tucked in a bay window is equipped with a walk-in pantry and cooking island.
- Laundry room has a chute from upstairs and sewing counter.
- Coffered ceiling master bedroom features a fireplace and walk-through wardrobe.
- Bonus room, with private staircase, provides an additional 367 square feet of living space.

First Floor	1,620 sq. ft.
Second Floor	1,064 sq. ft.
Total Living Area	2,684 sq. ft.

PRICE CODE: C

CUSTOMIZE IT!

ORDER TOLL FREE 1▪800▪533▪4350   **24-HOUR FAX ORDERING** 1▪800▪344▪4293

151

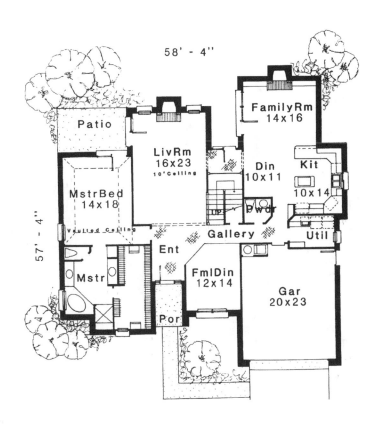

58' - 4''

57' - 4''

Patio

LivRm
16x23
10'Ceiling

FamilyRm
14x16

Din
10x11

Kit
10x14

MstrBed
14x18

Vaulted Ceiling

Pwdr

Gallery

Util

Mstr

Ent

FmlDin
12x14

Gar
20x23

Por

Total Living Area   2,721 sq. ft.

PRICE CODE: C

PLAN AM2206

◀ 68' ▶

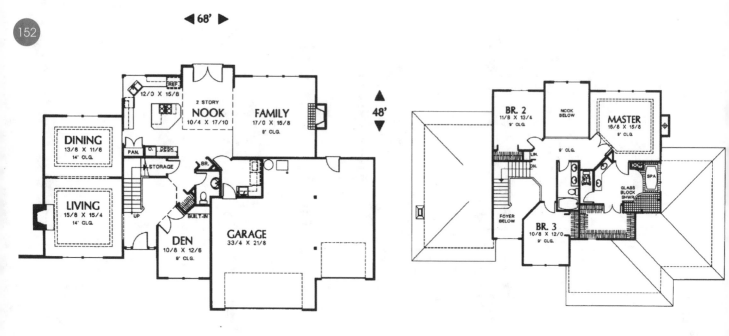

▲ 48' ▼

First Floor   1,600 sq. ft.
Second Floor   1,123 sq. ft.
Total Living Area   2,723 sq. ft.

PRICE CODE: C

CUSTOMIZE IT!

ORDER TOLL FREE   1 ▪ 800 ▪ 533 ▪ 4350   24-HOUR FAX ORDERING   1 ▪ 800 ▪ 344 ▪ 4293

153

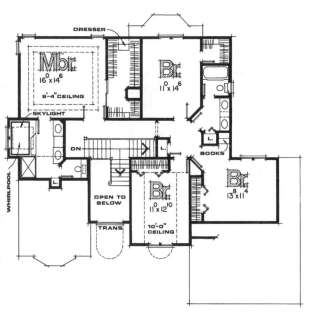

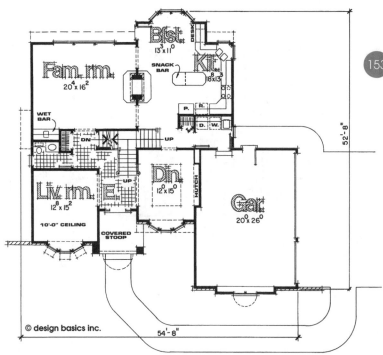

© design basics inc.

Features

Formal rooms with beautiful bayed windows flank volume entry.

Family room with wet bar shares see-thru fireplace with kitchen.

Large island kitchen with wrapping desk, pantry, corner sink and snack bar adjoins bayed breakfast area.

- Garage accesses home through laundry/mud room with utility sink and coat closet.
- Upstairs, double doors seen from entry open up into master bedroom.
- Built-in dresser in large master bedroom walk-in closet.
- Secondary bedrooms separated for privacy.

First Floor	1,392 sq. ft.
Second Floor	1,335 sq. ft.
Total Living Area	2,727 sq. ft.

PRICE CODE: D

154

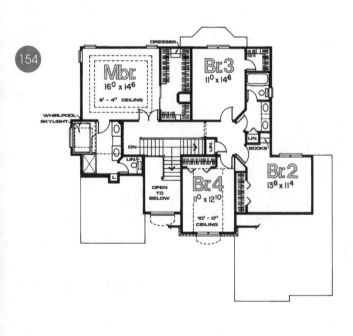

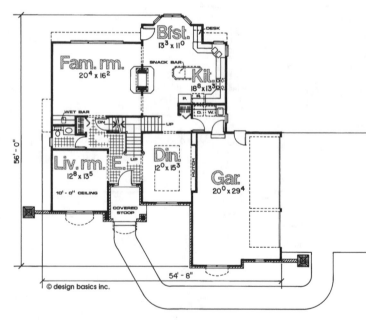

© design basics inc.

Features

- Full brick front elevation with brick quoins and wing walls with lights on piers.
- Repeating, segmented, arched-top windows endow this home with a dignified look.
- Formal rooms open to entry.
- Family room has wet bar, see-thru fireplace and large windows.

- Kitchen/breakfast area shares fireplace and includes pantry, wrapping desk and corner sink.
- Laundry room serves as mud entrance from garage.
- Master bath features double vanity and skylit whirlpool tub.

First Floor	1,400 sq.
Second Floor	1,335 sq.
Total Living Area	2,735 sq.

PRICE CODE: D

155

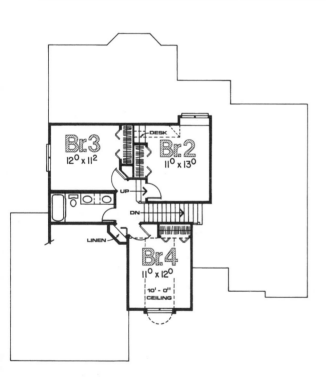

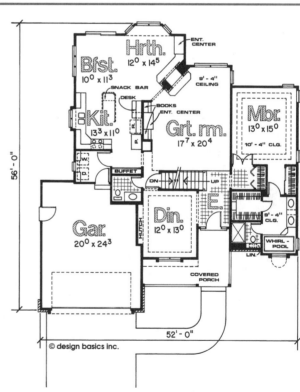

© design basics inc.

Features

Generous covered front porch.
Great room features bookcases, entertainment center and angled see-thru fireplace.
Island kitchen offers abundant amenities including built-in buffet serving counter for formal dining convenience.
Hearth room with bayed window and entertainment center.
Convenient utility entrance.

- Double doors into master bedroom with tiered ceiling
- Master dressing area with whirlpool under arched window.
- Upstairs, bedroom #4 has beautiful arched window with volume ceiling.

First Floor	1,595 sq. ft.
Second Floor	641 sq. ft.
Total Living Area	2,236 sq. ft.

PRICE CODE: D

◀ 70' ▶

SPA

BR. 4
11/0 X 12/4

INSTEAD OF VAULTING FAMILY RM. THIS AREA CAN BE BUILT AS 5TH BEDROOM WITH DORMER FACING THE REAR.

FAMILY RM. BELOW

DN.

LINEN

BR. 3
10/8 X 15/4

MASTER
13/0 X 17/0

FOYER BELOW

BR. 2
13/0 X 11/0

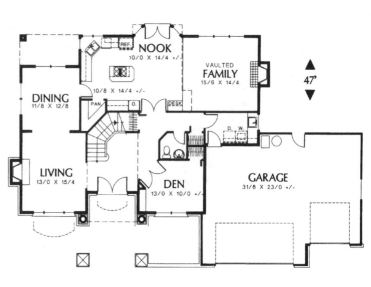

47'

REF.

NOOK
10/0 X 14/4

VAULTED FAMILY
15/6 X 14/4

DINING
11/8 X 12/8

10/8 X 14/4 +/-

PAN.

O.

DESK

D.W.

LIVING
13/0 X 15/4

DEN
13/0 X 10/0 +/-

GARAGE
31/8 X 23/0 +/-

First Floor	1,470 sq. ft.
Second Floor	1,269 sq. ft.
Total Living Area	2,739 sq. ft.

PRICE CODE: C

CUSTOMIZE IT!

ORDER TOLL FREE   1■800■533■4350   24-HOUR FAX ORDERING   1■800■344■4293

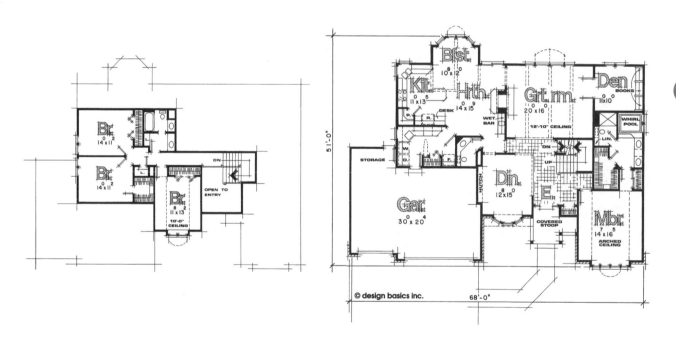

157

Features

- Formal dining room with bayed window and hutch space open to volume entry.
- See-thru fireplace serves hearth room and volume great room with arched windows and French doors to private den with bookcases.
- Kitchen includes island counter, corner walk-in pantry, planning desk, wet bar and bayed dinette

with cathedral ceiling.
- Convenient laundry/hobby area with sink, closet.
- Volume master bedroom shows off beautiful arched window arrangement and adjoins whirlpool bath.
- Compartmented bath for generous secondary bedrooms.

First Floor	**1,963 sq. ft.**
Second Floor	**778 sq. ft.**
Total Living Area	**2,741 sq. ft.**

PRICE CODE: D

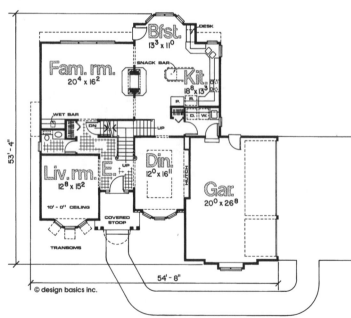

© design basics inc.

Features

- Economical lap siding enhanced by stone veneer at foundation and center gable.
- Repeated bay theme culminates with 2-story bay at center.
- Main level traffic patterns smoothed by T-shaped staircase.

- Powder bath located off of hard-surfaced entry.
- Family room secluded from entry for privacy.
- Kitchen with see-thru fireplace and snack bar adjoins bayed breakfast area.
- Master suite has luxury bath area and walk-in closet with built-in dresser.

First Floor	1,418 sq. f
Second Floor	1,344 sq. f
Total Living Area	2,762 sq. f

PRICE CODE: D

CUSTOMIZE IT!

ORDER TOLL FREE   1▪800▪533▪4350   24-HOUR FAX ORDERING   1▪800▪344▪4293

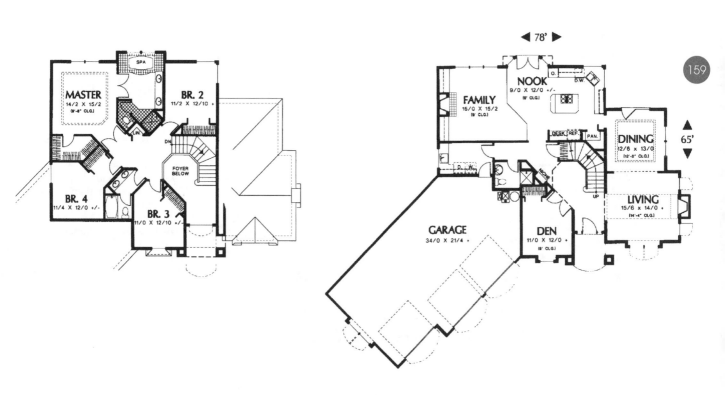

MASTER 14/2 X 15/2 (9'-8" CLG.)

BR. 2 11/2 X 12/10 +/-

BR. 4 11/4 X 12/0 +/-

BR. 3 11/0 X 12/10 +/-

SPA

FOYER BELOW

DN

◀ 78' ▶

159

FAMILY 15/0 X 15/2 (9' CLG.)

NOOK 9/0 X 12/0 +/- (9' CLG.)

DINING 12/6 x 13/0 (12'-6" CLG.)

65'

LIVING 15/6 X 14/0 +/- (14'-4" CLG.)

DESK REF. PAN.

UP

GARAGE 34/0 X 21/4

DEN 11/0 X 12/0 +/- (9' CLG.)

First Floor	1,592 sq. ft.
Second Floor	1,178 sq. ft.
Total Living Area	**2,770 sq. ft.**

PRICE CODE: C

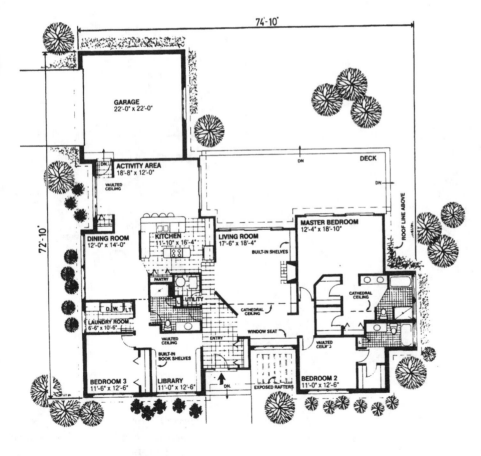

GARAGE
22'-0" x 22'-0"

ACTIVITY AREA
18'-8" x 12'-0"
VAULTED CEILING

DN.

DECK

DN

DINING ROOM
12'-0" x 14'-0"

KITCHEN
11'-10" x 16'-4"

LIVING ROOM
17'-6" x 18'-4"

MASTER BEDROOM
12'-4" x 18'-10"

BUILT-IN SHELVES

ROOF LINE ABOVE

PANTRY

D.W.

LT.

LAUNDRY ROOM
6'-6" x 10'-6"

UTILITY

CATHEDRAL CEILING

CATHEDRAL CEILING

VAULTED CEILING

WINDOW SEAT

VAULTED CEILING

BUILT-IN BOOK SHELVES

ENTRY

EXPOSED RAFTERS

BEDROOM 3
11'-6" x 12'-6"

LIBRARY
11'-0" x 12'-6"

DN.

BEDROOM 2
11'-0" x 12'-6"

74'-10"

72'-10"

160

Sunlight Views

Features

- Vaulted ceilings accent this one-story contemporary home.
- Foyer leads to living room on the right.
- Living room includes extras such as built-in window seats and book shelves and fireplace.
- Master bedroom at rear of right wing includes cathedral ceilings and large master bath with dressing area and walk-in closets.
- Second bedroom at right front has walk-in closets and private bath.
- Third bedroom located in left wing with access to full bath is adjacent to the library with built-in shelving.
- Centrally located kitchen includes cooking island, pantry, and snack bar that opens to adjacent activity area.

| Total Living Area | 2,773 sq. f |

PRICE CODE: C

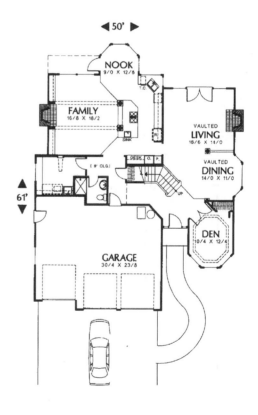

161

First Floor	**1,568 sq. ft.**
Second Floor	**1,227 sq. ft.**
Total Living Area	**2,795 sq. ft.**

PRICE CODE: C

162

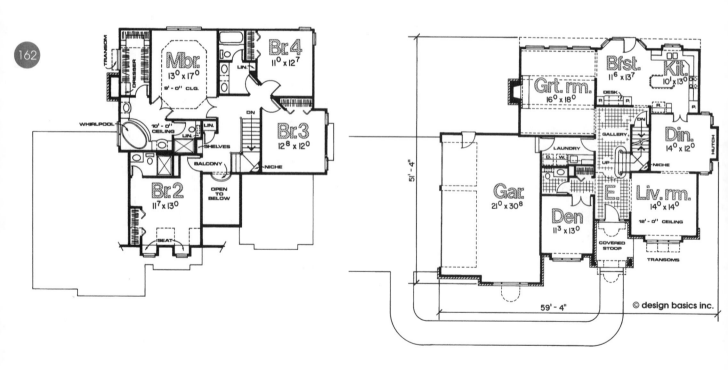

© design basics inc.

51' - 4"

59' - 4"

Features

- 9-foot main level walls.
- Gallery wall visible from entry.
- Tall boxed window in formal living room.
- French doors open into private den.
- Great room with large windows and intriguing fireplace.

- Desk, island counter and 2 pantries in kitchen.
- Upstairs, arched balcony overlooks entry below.
- Window seats and private bath for bedroom #2.
- Luxurious master dressing area with plant ledge above, his and her vanities and irresistible oval whirlpool.

First Floor	1,523 sq. ft
Second Floor	1,282 sq. f
Total Living Area	2,805 sq. f

PRICE CODE: D

CUSTOMIZE IT!

ORDER TOLL FREE 1 ▪ 800 ▪ 533 ▪ 4350   24-HOUR FAX ORDERING   1 ▪ 800 ▪ 344 ▪ 4293

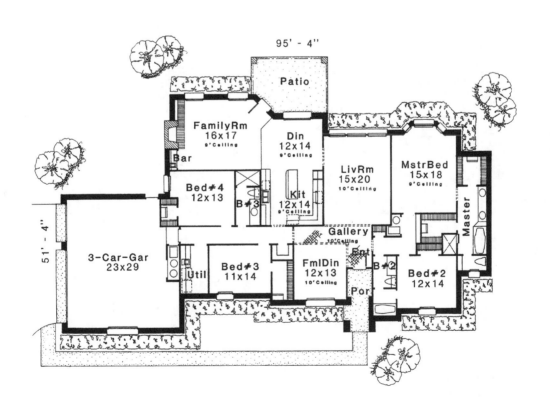

Total Living Area   2,805 sq. ft.

PRICE CODE: C

164

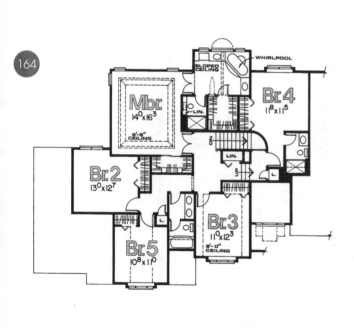

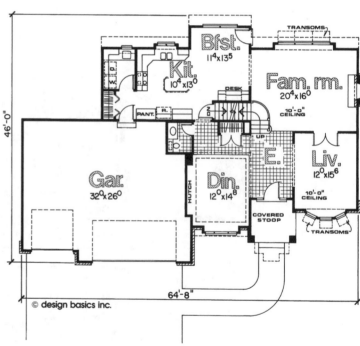

© design basics inc.

Features

- Dynamic elevation has instant curb appeal.
- Entry flanked by formal living room and dining room with hutch space.
- French doors between living room and family room add charm.
- Warming fireplace and sparkling picture/awning windows with transoms above highlight family room.
- Island kitchen and bright dinette features lazy

Susan, planning desk and pantry.
- Window-lit laundry has soaking sink.
- Four secondary bedrooms upstairs, bedroom #4 has private bath.
- Luxurious master suite with dynamic vaulted ceiling and two walk-in closets.
- Dressing area with corner whirlpool and his and her vanities.

First Floor	1,335 sq. f
Second Floor	1,475 sq. f
Total Living Area	2,810 sq. f

PRICE CODE: D

CUSTOMIZE IT!

ORDER TOLL FREE 1▪800▪533▪4350   **24-HOUR FAX ORDERING** 1▪800▪344▪4293

165

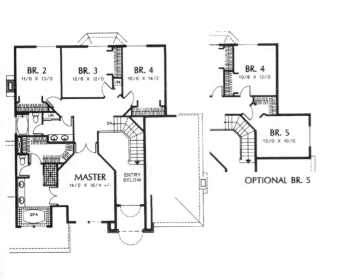

BR. 2
11/0 X 13/0

BR. 3
12/6 X 12/0

BR. 4
10/6 X 14/2

BR. 4
10/6 X 12/0

BR. 5
13/0 X 10/0

MASTER
14/0 X 18/4 +/-

ENTRY BELOW

SPA

OPTIONAL BR. 5

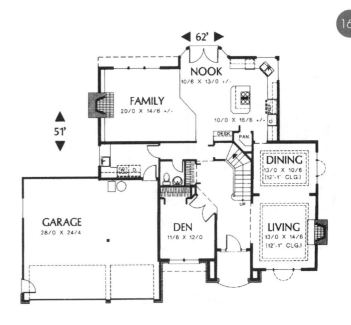

◀ 62' ▶

NOOK
10/6 X 13/0 +/-

FAMILY
20/0 X 14/6 +/-

10/0 X 16/6 +/-

DESK. PAN.

51'

DINING
13/0 X 10/6
(12'-1" CLG.)

UP

GARAGE
28/0 X 24/4

DEN
11/8 X 12/0

LIVING
13/0 X 14/6
(12'-1" CLG.)

First Floor	1,547 sq. ft.
Second Floor	1,265 sq. ft.
Total Living Area	2,812 sq. ft.
Optional Bedroom 5	154 sq. ft.

PRICE CODE: C

CUSTOMIZE IT!

ORDER TOLL FREE 1▪800▪533▪4350   24-HOUR FAX ORDERING   1▪800▪344▪4293

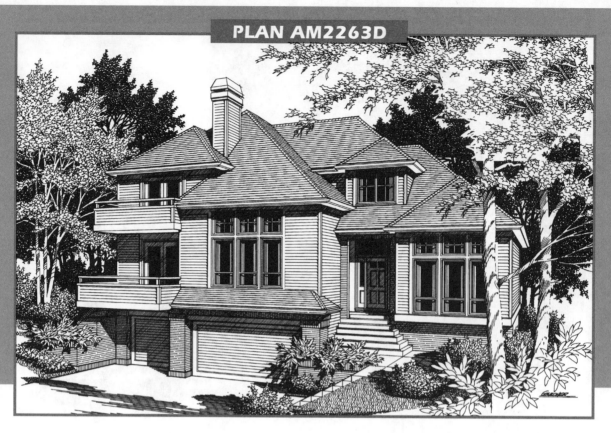

166

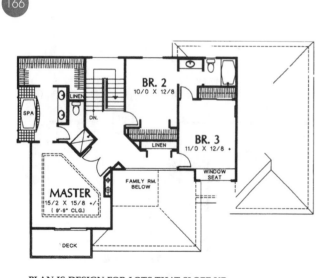

**PLAN IS DESIGN FOR LOTS THAT SLOPE UP
APPROX 8' IN THE DEPTH OF THE PLAN**

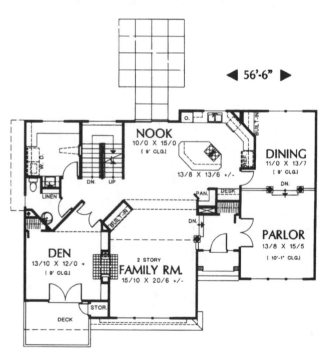

◀ 56'-6" ▶

38'

3 CAR GARAGE UNDER

Lower Floor	102 sq. ft.
First Floor	1,713 sq. ft.
Second Floor	998 sq. ft.
Total Living Area	2,813 sq. ft.

PRICE CODE: C

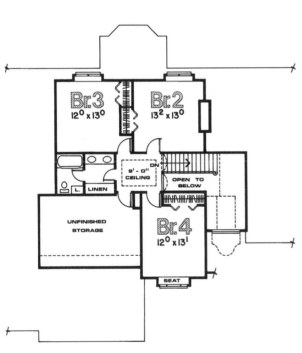

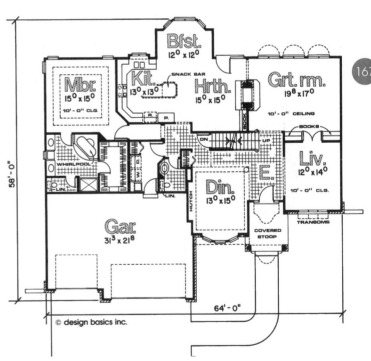

167

Features

- Brick and stucco accents curb appeal.
- Elegant entry surveys formal living room with volume ceiling and bayed window dining room with hutch space.
- Window-brightened great room includes see-thru fireplace and built-in bookcases.
- Gourmet kitchen, bayed dinette and hearth room with see-thru fireplace and bookcase offer

enhancements to family living.
- Secondary bedrooms enjoy compartmented bath with dual lavs and huge linen cabinet.
- Secluded main floor master suite features tiered ceiling, walk-in closet, luxury bath with whirlpool and his and her vanities.

First Floor	2,073 sq. ft.
Second Floor	741 sq. ft.
Total Living Area	2,814 sq. ft.

PRICE CODE: D

PLAN AM2237P

168

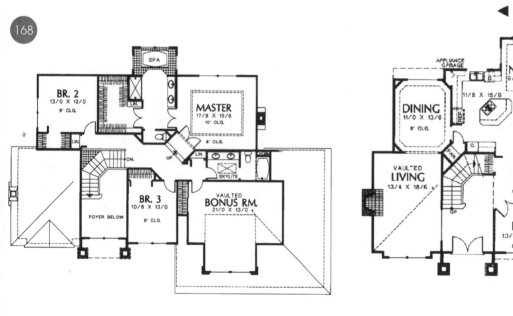

◀ 68' ▶

51'

SPA

BR. 2
13/0 X 12/0
9' CLG.

LIN.

MASTER
17/8 X 15/6
10' CLG.

8' CLG.

DN.   UP

LIN.

SKYLITE

BR. 3
10/8 X 13/0
9' CLG.

FOYER BELOW

VAULTED
BONUS RM.
21/0 X 13/0 ±
9' CLG.

APPLIANCE
GARAGE

NOOK
9/4 X 11/4
10' CLG.

DINING
11/0 X 13/6
9' CLG.

11/8 X 15/6

FAMILY RM.
17/8 X 15/6 +/-
10' CLG.

DESK

WET BAR

VAULTED
LIVING
13/4 X 18/6

BUILT-IN

DEN
10/8 X 11/10
9' CLG.

W.D.

GARAGE
26/0 X 28/6 ±

First Floor	1,618 sq. ft.
Second Floor	1,212 sq. ft.
Total Living Area	2,830 sq. ft.
Bonus Room	+376 sq. ft.

PRICE CODE: C

◀ 50' ▶
(40' - 2 CAR)

169

60'-6"

First Floor	1,466 sq. ft.
Second Floor	1,369 sq. ft.
Total Living Area	2,835 sq. ft.

PRICE CODE: C

170

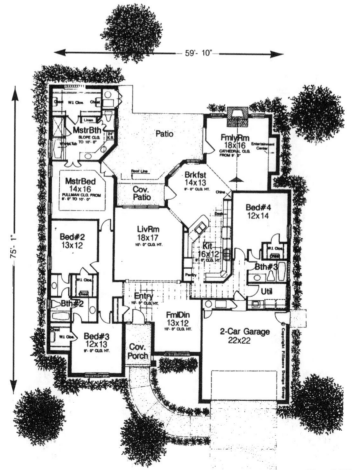

59'- 10"

75'- 1"

Total Living Area   2,843 sq. ft.

PRICE CODE: C

171

3-Car-Gar
24x32

Patio Area

BrkfstRm
13x10
10"Clg.

Patio Area

FamilyRm
16x17
10"Clg.

MstrBed
17x14

LivRm
17x15
10"Clg.

Kit
13x14
10"Clg.

Util
8'Clg.

68' - 4"

Study
11x11

Ent/Gallery
11"Clg.

FmlDin
12x13
11'Clg.

Bed#3
12x12
10"Clg.

Bed#4
12x12
8'Clg.

Bed#2
14x11

Total Living Area   **2,858 sq. ft.**

PRICE CODE: C

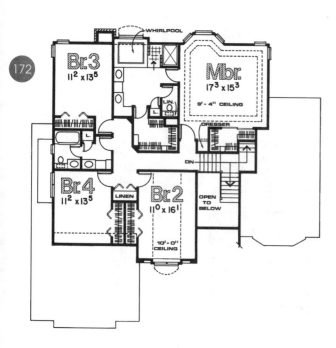

172

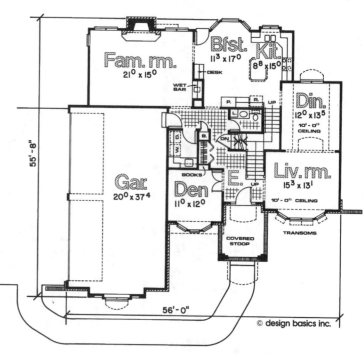

© design basics inc.

Features

- Brick wing walls, stucco accents and trim details enrich elevation.
- Entry views bayed-window living room and French-doored den with built-in bookcase and bayed window.
- Gourmet kitchen/breakfast area has wrapping counters, island and pantry.
- Family room with exquisite fireplace and wet

bar/servery.
- Secondary bedrooms share nearby bath.
- Master suite enriched by bayed sitting area, built-in dresser and walk-in closet.
- Luxurious dressing area with whirlpool, glass block, dual lavs with make-up space and a second walk-in closet.

First Floor	**1,501 sq. ft.**
Second Floor	**1,389 sq. ft.**
Total Living Area	**2,890 sq. ft.**

PRICE CODE: D

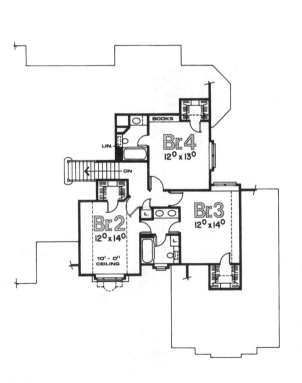

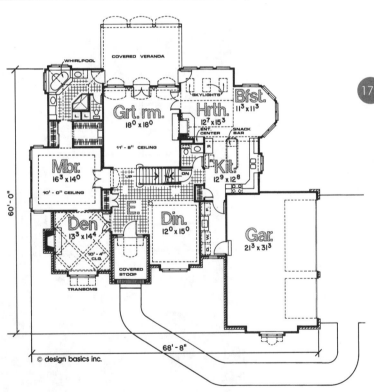

© design basics inc.

Features

- Majestic elevation with side-load garage combines stucco, brick and elegant details for instant curb appeal.
- Entry surveys great room and dining room.
- Intriguing ceiling in den with cozy fireplace.
- Open, formal dining room extends entertaining space.
- Elegant great room with see-thru fireplace and French doors to covered veranda.
- Lovely hearth room features three skylights, a wall of three large picture/awning windows and an entertainment center.
- Sunny bayed dinette and kitchen with island, snack bar, wrapping counters and pantry enhance daily family living.
- Three secondary bedrooms upstairs, each with a walk-in closet and ample bathroom space; bedroom #4 has built-in bookcase.
- Main level sumptuous master suite affords luxury accommodations with two closets, whirlpool tub, his and her vanities and access to a covered veranda.

First Floor	**2,084 sq. ft.**
Second Floor	**848 sq. ft.**
Total Living Area	**2,932 sq. ft.**

PRICE CODE: D

CUSTOMIZE IT!

ORDER TOLL FREE   1 ▪ 800 ▪ 533 ▪ 4350   24-HOUR FAX ORDERING   1 ▪ 800 ▪ 344 ▪ 4293

173

PLAN FD7847-LA

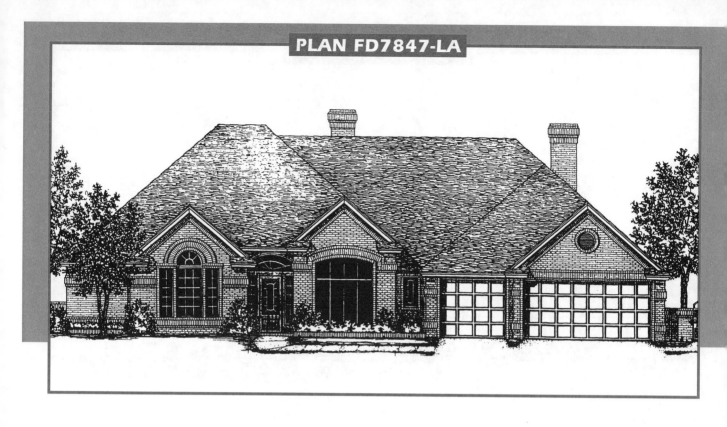

174

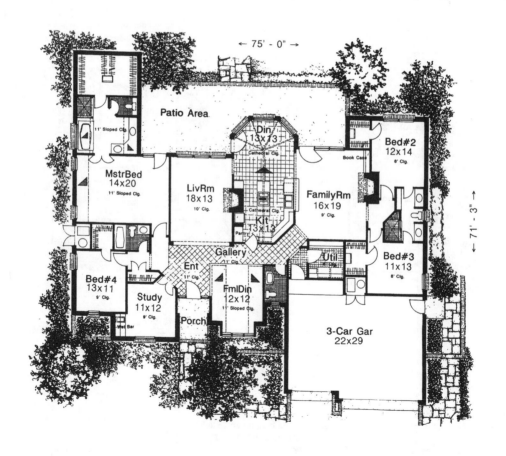

Total Living Area   2,932 sq. ft.

PRICE CODE: C

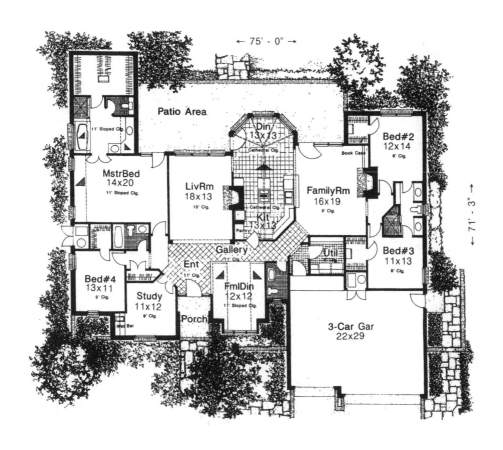

← 75' - 0" →

← 71' - 3" →

Patio Area

Din
13x13
Cathedral Clg.

Bed#2
12x14
8' Clg.

Book Case

MstrBed
14x20
11' Sloped Clg.

LivRm
18x13
10' Clg.

FamilyRm
16x19
9' Clg.

Kit
13x13

11' Sloped Clg.

Pantry

Gallery
11' Clg.

Util

Bed#3
11x13
8' Clg.

Ent
11' Clg.

Bed#4
13x11
9' Clg.

Study
11x12
9' Clg.

FmlDin
12x12
11' Sloped Clg.

Porch

Wet Bar

3-Car Gar
22x29

Total Living Area   2,932 sq. ft.

PRICE CODE: C

CUSTOMIZE IT!

176

Total Living Area 2,945 sq. ft.

PRICE CODE: C

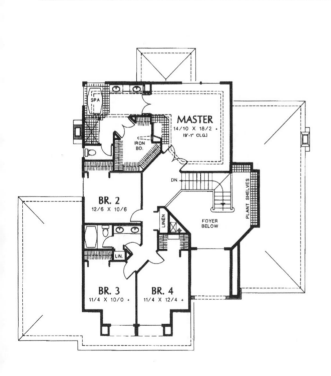

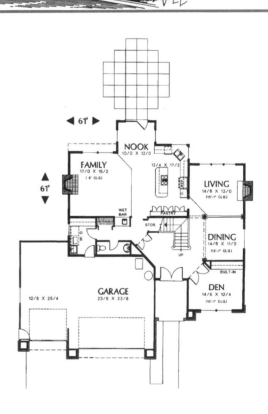

First Floor	1,632 sq. ft.
Second Floor	1,334 sq. ft.
Total Living Area	2,966 sq. ft.

PRICE CODE: C

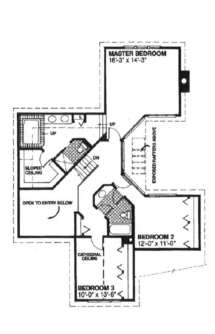

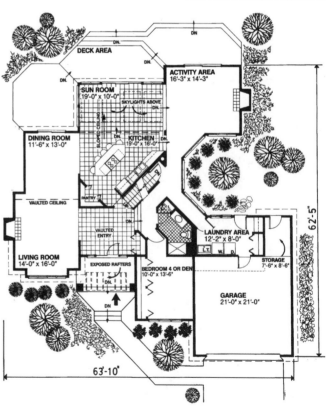

Garden Sanctuary

Features

- Bright and spacious living are the rule in this contemporary two-story.
- Sunlit, vaulted entrance leads to living room/dining room combination, featuring a fireplace and vaulted ceiling.
- Large sunken sun room with skylights and sloped

ceilings include a garden area off the family area.
- A cathedral ceiling in one of the bedrooms provides an added touch.
- Second bedroom overlooks garden area.
- Master bedroom features adjacent spa and separate shower area.

First Floor	1,886 sq. ft.
Second Floor	1,127 sq. ft.
Total Living Area	**3,013 sq. ft.**

PRICE CODE: C

CUSTOMIZE IT!

ORDER TOLL FREE **1 ▪ 800 ▪ 533 ▪ 4350**   24-HOUR FAX ORDERING **1 ▪ 800 ▪ 344 ▪ 4293**

MASTER BEDROOM
6'-3" x 14'-3"

SLOPED CEILING

UP

DN

DN

OPEN TO ENTRY BELOW

EXPOSED RAFTERS ABOVE

BEDROOM 2
12'-0" x 11'-0"

BEDROOM 3
10'-0" x 13'-6"

SECOND FLOOR

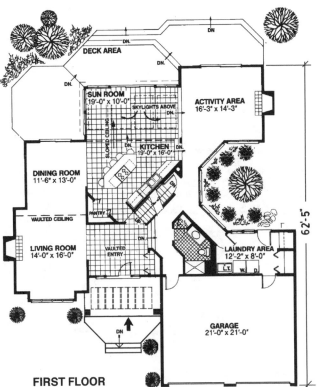

DECK AREA

DN.

DN.

DN.

SUN ROOM
19'-0" x 10'-0"

SKYLIGHTS ABOVE

DN.

ACTIVITY AREA
16'-3" x 14'-3"

KITCHEN
19'-0" x 16'-0"

DINING ROOM
11'-6" x 13'-0"

SLOPED CEILING

PANTRY

VAULTED CEILING

LIVING ROOM
14'-0" x 16'-0"

VAULTED ENTRY

DN.

LAUNDRY AREA
12'-2" x 8'-0"

L.T. W. D.

DN.

GARAGE
21'-0" x 21'-0"

62'-5"

FIRST FLOOR

179

Contemporary Retreat

Features

- Unique two-story design.
- Exterior features overhangs, gabled vertical windows, multiple roof lines for maximum interest.
- Large sunken sun room with skylights and sloped ceiling.
- Garden area off the family room enables you to enjoy natural surroundings all year round.
- First-floor bedroom or den with bath.
- Second floor features two bedrooms with bath and master bedroom with deluxe bath.
- Vaulted and cathedral ceilings add to the magnificence of this design.

First Floor	1,699 sq. ft.
Second Floor	1,127 sq. ft.
Total Living Area	**2,826 sq. ft.**

PRICE CODE: C

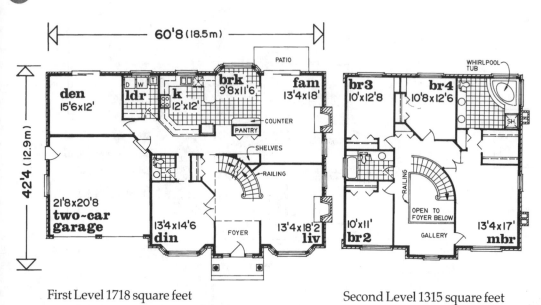

First Level 1718 square feet

Second Level 1315 square feet

Features

- Kitchen, with pantry and abundant counter space, is open to the breakfast bay and family room.
- Sliding glass access to the patio and fireplace makes the family room an ideal gathering spot.
- Game room can easily be used as an office, studio or guest room.
- Bay windows adorn the living and dining rooms.
- Curved staircase ascends to a railed gallery and library which views the foyer below.
- Master bedroom features a walk-in wardrobe and lavish ensuite with twin vanity and whirlpool spa.
- Library, which opens to the master bedroom, is an ideal computer station.

First Floor	1,718 sq. f
Second Floor	1,315 sq. f
Total Living Area	3,033 sq. f

PRICE CODE: C

CUSTOMIZE IT!

ORDER TOLL FREE 1■800■533■4350   24-HOUR FAX ORDERING   1■800■344■4293

PLAN DB940

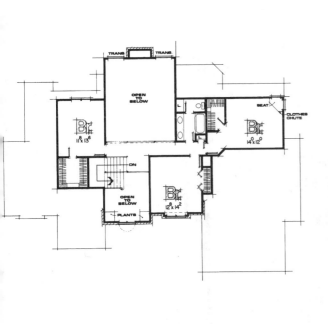

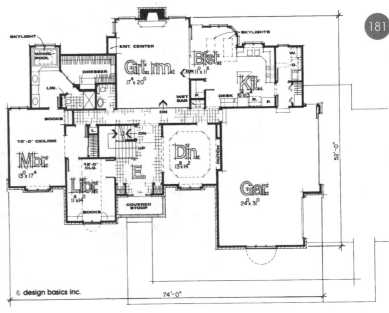

© design basics inc.

Features

- 2-story-high entry with plant shelves atop dual coat closets.
- Wet bar convenient to dining room with hutch space.
- French doors open into library with volume ceiling and built-in bookcases .
- Sunken great room with sloped ceiling and built-in entertainment center spotlights beautiful fireplace .

- Master bedroom with built-in bookcase adjoins skylit bath area with double vanity, large walk-in closet with mirrored bypass doors plus built-in dresser and 2-person whirlpool tub.
- Secondary bedrooms share hall bath.

First Floor	**2,078 sq. ft.**
Second Floor	**960 sq. ft.**
Total Living Area	**3,038 sq. ft.**

PRICE CODE: D

PLAN FD6735-L

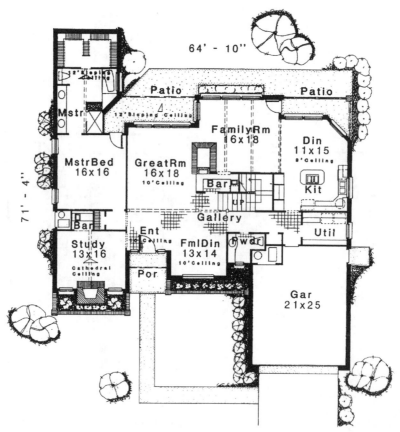

64' - 10''

71' - 4''

Patio

Patio

Mstr

12' Sloping Ceiling

MstrBed
16x16

FamilyRm
16x18

Din
11x15
8'Ceiling

GreatRm
16x18
10'Ceiling

Bar

Kit

Bar

Gallery

Util

Ent

FmlDin
13x14
10'Ceiling

Pwdr

Study
13x16
Cathedral
Ceiling

Por

Gar
21x25

Total Living Area 3,040 sq. ft.

PRICE CODE: C

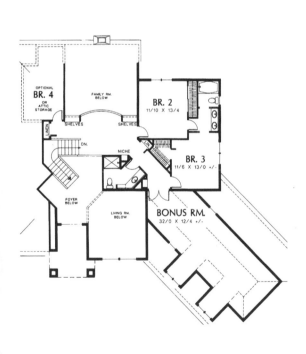

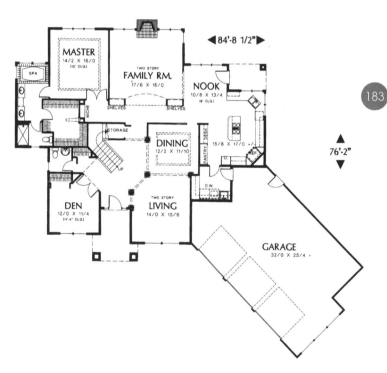

183

IF OPTIONAL 4TH BR USED,
MASTER BEDROOM BELOW WILL BE
LIMITED TO 9' CEILING

First Floor	2,270 sq. ft.
Second Floor	788 sq. ft.
Total Living Area	3,058 sq. ft.
Bonus Room	+520 sq. ft.
4th BR.	+168 sq. ft.

PRICE CODE: C

PLAN DB909

184

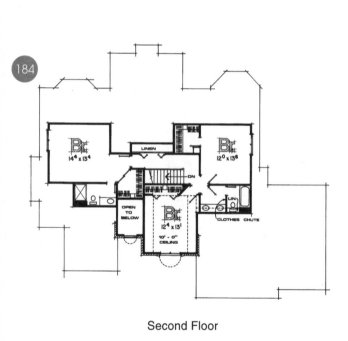

Second Floor

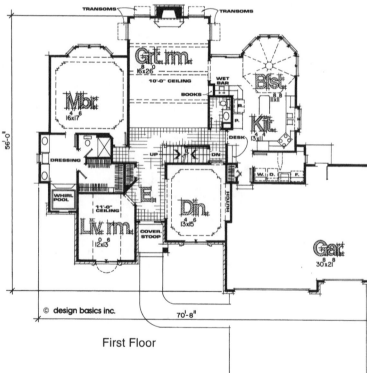

First Floor

Features

- Formal entertaining rooms flank volume entry for elegant first impressions.
- Expansive view from entry reveals great room with beamed ceiling, bookcase and fireplace framed by large windows.
- Powder bath discretely located.
- Gourmet kitchen with island counter, corner range, wrapping counters and planning desk adjoins semi-gazebo breakfast area with vaulted ceiling.

- Wet bar convenient to great room and kitchen/breakfast .
- Master bedroom with gracious ceiling detail and bayed windows adjoins bath area featuring large walk-in closet, double vanity and 2-person whirlpool tub .
- Third bedroom has beautiful arched transom window and volume ceiling.

First Floor	**2,048 sq. ft**
Second Floor	**1,027 sq. ft**
Total Living Area	**3,075 sq. ft**

PRICE CODE: D

185

Total Living Area   **3,101 sq. ft.**

PRICE CODE: C

CUSTOMIZE IT!

ORDER TOLL FREE   1▪800▪533▪4350   24-HOUR FAX ORDERING   1▪800▪344▪4293

186

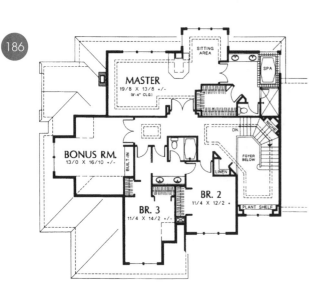

First Floor	1,779 sq. ft.
Second Floor	1,335 sq. ft.
Total Living Area	3,114 sq. ft.
Office	+209 sq. ft
Bonus Room	+270 sq. ft.

PRICE CODE: C

187

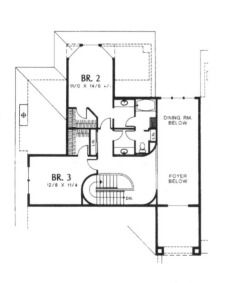

BR. 2
11/0 X 14/6 +/-

DINING RM.
BELOW

BR. 3
12/8 X 11/4

FOYER
BELOW

DN.

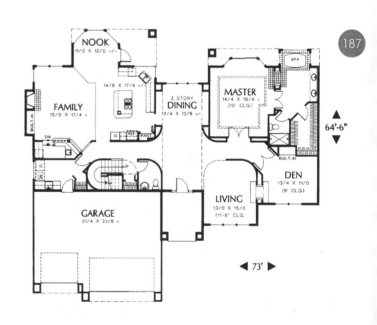

NOOK
11/0 X 12/0 +/-

14/6 X 17/4 +/-

SPA

MASTER
14/4 X 16/4
(10' CLG.)

FAMILY
15/0 X 17/4

2 STORY
DINING
13/4 X 13/8

BUILT-IN

BUILT-IN

DN.

UP

DEN
13/4 X 11/0
(9' CLG.)

GARAGE
31/4 X 21/8

LIVING
13/0 X 15/0
(11'-6" CLG.)

64'-6"

◀ 73' ▶

First Floor	2,375 sq. ft.
Second Floor	762 sq. ft.
Total Living Area	3,137 sq. ft.

PRICE CODE: C

188

BONUS RM. (W/ OPTIONAL BATH)

BR. 2 11/0 X 13/2

BR. 3 14/4 X 10/10 +/-

BR. 4 14/6 X 10/10 +/-

MASTER 13/6 X 15/8

FOYER BELOW

SPA

LIN

DN.

DN.

◄ 69' ►

GARAGE 23/8 X 32/4 +

NOOK 11/0 X 13/0 +/-

12/10 X 12/8

FAMILY 17/0 X 18/6 +/-

REF.

PAN.

DESK

SHOP 9/8 X 10/0 +

W. D.

BAR BAR

UP

DINING 15/0 X 11/0

DEN/BR. 5 12/4 X 11/0 +/-

BUILT-IN

LIVING 13/6 X 15/6

55' ▲▼

First Floor	1,746 sq. ft.
Second Floor	1,396 sq. ft.
Total Living Area	3,142 sq. ft.
Bonus Room	+584 sq. ft.

PRICE CODE: C

CUSTOMIZE IT!

ORDER TOLL FREE   1■800■533■4350   24-HOUR FAX ORDERING   1■800■344■4293

PLAN AM2329B

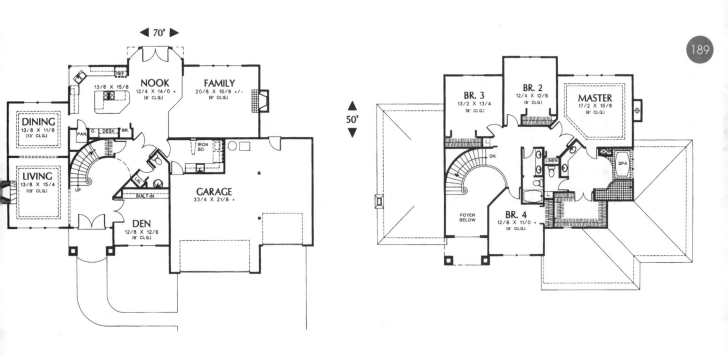

DINING
13/8 X 11/8
[13' CLG.]

LIVING
13/8 X 15/4
[13' CLG.]

NOOK
12/4 X 14/0 +
(9' CLG.)

FAMILY
20/8 X 15/8 +/-
(9' CLG.)

13/6 X 15/8

PAN. D. DESK. BR.

IRON BD.

UP

BOLT-IN

GARAGE
33/4 X 21/8 +

DEN
12/8 X 12/6
(9' CLG.)

◄ 70' ►

▲ 50' ▼

BR. 3
13/2 X 13/4
(9' CLG.)

BR. 2
12/4 X 12/6
(9' CLG.)

MASTER
17/2 X 15/8
(9' CLG.)

DN.

LINEN

SPA

FOYER BELOW

BR. 4
12/8 X 11/0 +
(9' CLG.)

First Floor 1,764 sq. ft.
Second Floor 1,393 sq. ft.
Total Living Area 3,157 sq. ft.

PRICE CODE: C

CUSTOMIZE IT!

ORDER TOLL FREE 1▪800▪533▪4350 24-HOUR FAX ORDERING 1▪800▪344▪4293

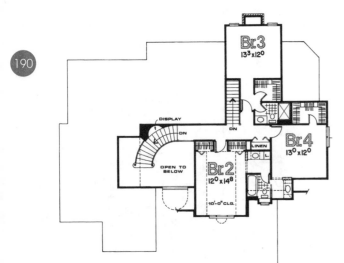

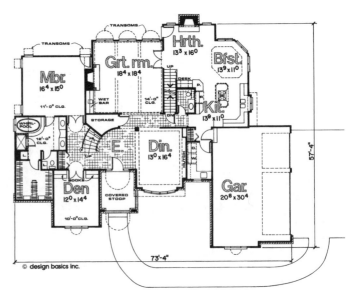

© design basics inc.

Features

- Spacious formal entry with spectacular curving staircase, 9-foot main level walls.
- Arched transom above double doors into volume den with built-in bookcases and arched window.
- Repeating arched windows out the back of the large great room.
- Second fireplace in hearth room open to dinette/kitchen area.

- Amenities abound in gourmet kitchen with cooktop in island.
- Separate informal staircase.
- Master bedroom retreat with private back door and luxurious dressing area featuring oval whirlpool and large walk-in closet.
- Generous closets and baths for secondary bedrooms.

First Floor 2,252 sq
Second Floor 920 sq
Total Living Area 3,172 sq

PRICE CODE: E

CUSTOMIZE IT!

ORDER TOLL FREE 1■800■533■4350   24-HOUR FAX ORDERING   1■800■344■4293

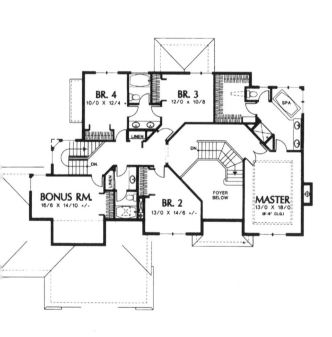

BR. 4
10/0 X 12/4

BR. 3
12/0 x 10/8

SPA

LINEN

DN.

DN.

LINEN

BONUS RM.
16/6 X 14/10 +/-

BR. 2
13/0 X 14/6 +/-

FOYER
BELOW

MASTER
13/0 X 18/0
(8'-9" CLG.)

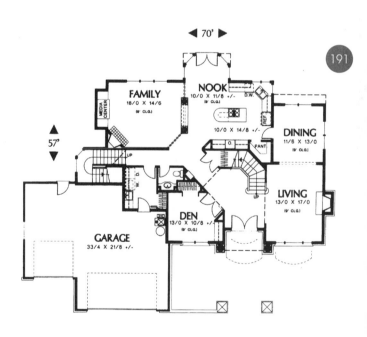

◄ 70' ►

191

FAMILY
18/0 X 14/6
(9' CLG.)

NOOK
10/0 X 11/8 +/-
(9' CLG.)

D.W.

MEDIA
CENTER

REF.

DINING
11/8 X 13/0
(9' CLG.)

57'

UP

PANT.

W D

DEN
13/0 X 10/8
(9' CLG.)

UP

UP

LIVING
13/0 X 17/0
(9' CLG.)

GARAGE
33/4 X 21/8 +/-

First Floor	1,763 sq. ft.
Second Floor	1,469 sq. ft.
Total Living Area	3,232 sq. ft.
Bonus Room	+256 sq. ft.

PRICE CODE: D

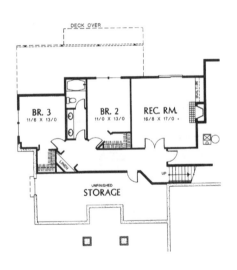

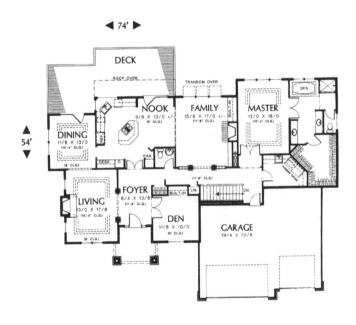

First Floor	2,188 sq. ft
Second Floor	1,049 sq. ft
Total Living Area	3,237 sq. ft

PRICE CODE: D

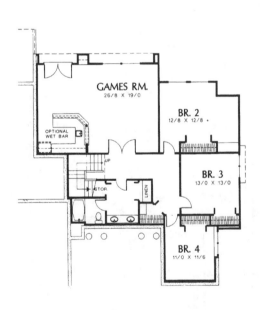

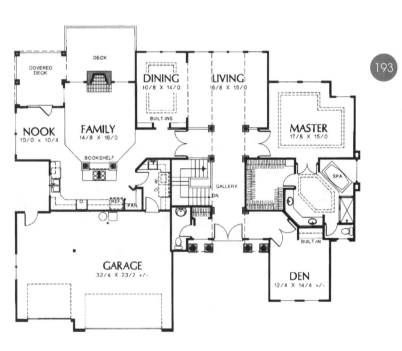

First Floor	2,196 sq. ft.
Lower Level	1,542 sq. ft.
Total Living Area	3,738 sq. ft.

PRICE CODE: E

CUSTOMIZE IT!

ORDER TOLL FREE 1•800•533•4350   24-HOUR FAX ORDERING 1•800•344•4293

◀ 72' ▶

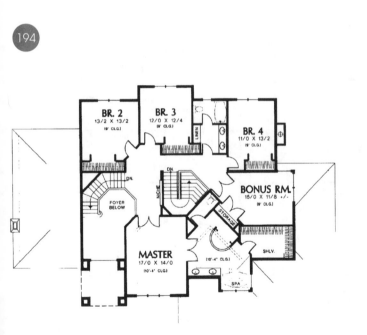

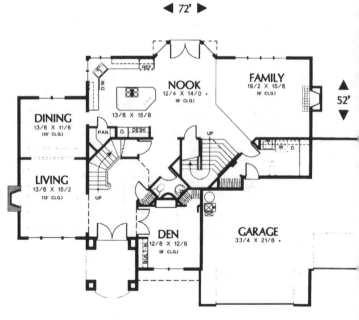

First Floor	1,915 sq. ft.
Second Floor	1,469 sq. ft.
Total Living Area	3,384 sq. ft
Bonus Room	+202 sq. ft

PRICE CODE: D

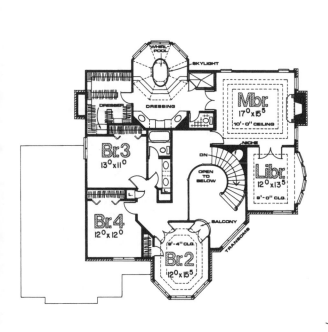

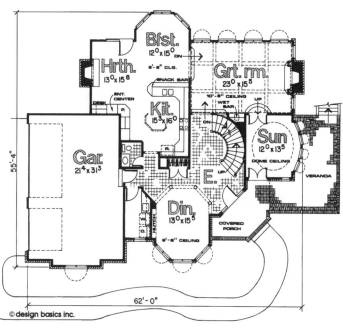

© design basics inc.

195

Features

Enter on angle to view spectacular curving staircase and columns defining volume dining room.

Bayed dining room highlights arched windows and hutch space.

Domed ceiling in sunroom with beautiful bowed windows.

Sun room provides access to extensive veranda and covered porch area.

• Enviable kitchen boasts central island, peninsula snack bar and generous cabinet space.

• French doors open to bedroom #2 with intriguing design and balcony admiring entry.

• Master dressing area features unique gazebo ceiling with skylight over oval whirlpool, his and her lavs and large walk-in closet with dresser.

First Floor	**1,719 sq. ft.**
Second Floor	**1,688 sq. ft.**
Total Living Area	**3,407 sq. ft.**

PRICE CODE: E

CUSTOMIZE IT!

ORDER TOLL FREE   1■800■533■4350   24-HOUR FAX ORDERING   1■800■344■4293

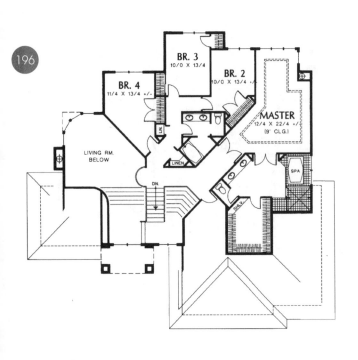

First Floor	1,894 sq. ft.
Second Floor	1,544 sq. ft.
Total Living Area	3,438 sq. ft.

PRICE CODE: D

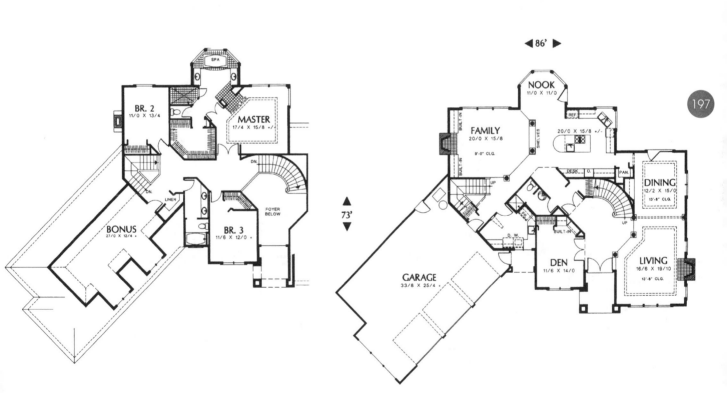

◄ 86' ►

▲
73'
▼

NOOK 11/0 X 11/0

FAMILY 20/0 X 15/8 9'-0" CLG.

20/0 X 15/8 +/-

REF.

SHELVES

BUILT-IN

BUILT-IN

DESK D. PAN.

DINING 12/2 X 15/0 13'-4" CLG.

UP

D. W.

BUILT-IN

DEN 11/6 X 14/0

LIVING 16/6 X 19/10 13'-8" CLG.

GARAGE 33/8 X 25/4

BR. 2 11/0 X 13/4

MASTER 17/4 X 15/8 +/-

SPA

DN.

DN.

LINEN

BONUS 27/0 X 12/4 +

BR. 3 11/6 X 12/0 +

FOYER BELOW

DN.

First Floor	**2,148 sq. ft.**
Second Floor	**1,300 sq. ft.**
Total Living Area	**3,448 sq. ft.**

PRICE CODE: D

CUSTOMIZE IT!

ORDER TOLL FREE 1■800■533■4350   **24-HOUR FAX ORDERING** 1■800■344■4293

198

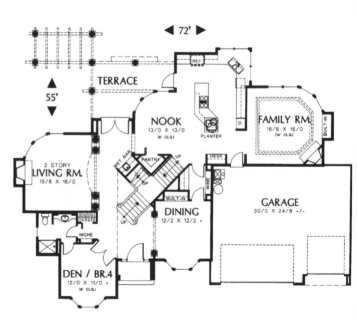

First Floor	1,920 sq. ft.
Second Floor	1,552 sq. ft.
Total Living Area	3,472 sq. ft.
Bonus Room	+252 sq. ft

PRICE CODE: D

199

2ND FLOOR

- BEDROOM 2
  11'-0" X 14'-4"
  9' CH
- BATH
- BEDROOM 3
  11'-0" X 14'-0"
  9' CH
- W.I.C.
- W.I.C.
- BALCONY
- DN
- MEDIA ROOM
  12'-4" X 14'-8"
  9' CH
- TV
- DN
- BATH
- BEDROOM 4
  11'-4" X 12'-0"
  9' CH
- W.I.C.
- UNFINISHED

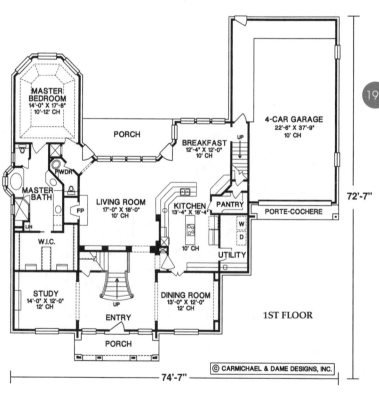

- MASTER BEDROOM
  14'-0" X 17'-8"
  10'-12' CH
- PORCH
- BREAKFAST
  12'-4" X 12'-0"
  10' CH
- UP
- 4-CAR GARAGE
  22'-6" X 37'-9"
  10' CH
- MASTER BATH
- PWDR
- LIVING ROOM
  17'-0" X 18'-0"
  10' CH
- FP
- KITCHEN
  13'-4" X 18'-4"
- PANTRY
- W
- D
- UTILITY
- PORTE-COCHERE
- LIN
- W.I.C.
- STUDY
  14'-0" X 12'-0"
  12' CH
- UP
- DINING ROOM
  13'-0" X 12'-0"
  12' CH
- ENTRY
- PORCH
- 10' CH
- 1ST FLOOR
- 72'-7"
- 74'-7"

© CARMICHAEL & DAME DESIGNS, INC.

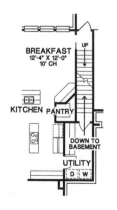

- BREAKFAST
  12'-4" X 12'-0"
  10' CH
- UP
- KITCHEN
- PANTRY
- DOWN TO BASEMENT
- UTILITY
- D W

First Floor	2,289 sq. ft.
Second Floor	1,204 sq. ft.
Total Living Area	3,493 sq. ft.

PRICE CODE: F

200

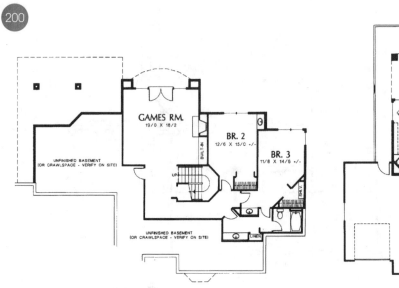

GAMES RM.
19/0 X 18/2

BR. 2
12/6 X 15/0 +/-

BR. 3
11/8 X 14/6 +/-

UNFINISHED BASEMENT
(OR CRAWLSPACE - VERIFY ON SITE)

UNFINISHED BASEMENT
(OR CRAWLSPACE - VERIFY ON SITE)

LINEN

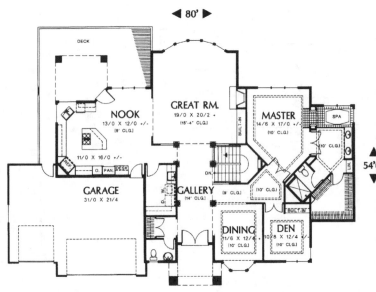

◄ 80' ►

DECK

NOOK
13/0 X 12/0 +/-
(9' CLG.)

GREAT RM.
19/0 X 20/2 +/-
(15'-4" CLG.)

MASTER
14/6 X 17/0 +/-
(10' CLG.)

SPA

11/0 X 16/0 +/-

GARAGE
31/0 X 21/4

GALLERY
(14' CLG.)

DINING
11/6 X 12/4
(10' CLG.)

DEN
10/8 X 12/4
(10' CLG.)

54'6"

Lower floor	1,324 sq. ft.
First Floor	2,219 sq. ft.
Total Living Area	3,543 sq. ft.

PRICE CODE: D

CUSTOMIZE IT!

ORDER TOLL FREE 1■800■533■4350   24-HOUR FAX ORDERING   1■800■344■4293

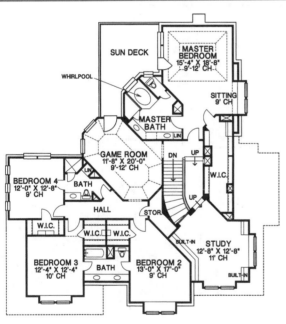

SUN DECK

MASTER BEDROOM
15'-4" X 18'-8"
9'-12' CH.

WHIRLPOOL

SITTING
9' CH

MASTER BATH

LIN

DN UP

GAME ROOM
11'-8" X 20'-0"
9'-12' CH

W.I.C.

BEDROOM 4
12'-0" X 12'-8"
9' CH

LIN

BATH

HALL

UP

STOR.

W.I.C.

W.I.C. W.I.C.

BUILT-IN

STUDY
12'-8" X 12'-8"
11' CH

BEDROOM 3
12'-4" X 12'-4"
10' CH

BATH

BEDROOM 2
13'-0" X 17'-0"
9' CH

BUILT-IN

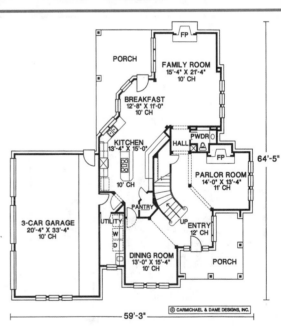

PORCH

FAMILY ROOM
15'-4" X 21'-4"
10' CH

FP

BREAKFAST
12'-8" X 11'-0"
10' CH

KITCHEN
13'-4" X 15'-0"

PWDR

HALL

FP

10' CH

PARLOR ROOM
14'-0" X 13'-4"
11' CH

3-CAR GARAGE
20'-4" X 33'-4"
10' CH

UTILITY

W
D

PANTRY

UP

ENTRY
12' CH

DINING ROOM
13'-0" X 15'-4"
10' CH

PORCH

64'-5"

© CARMICHAEL & DAME DESIGNS, INC.

59'-3"

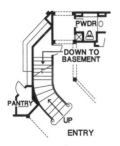

PWDR

DOWN TO BASEMENT

PANTRY

UP

ENTRY

First Floor	1,550 sq. ft.
Second Floor	2,102 sq. ft.
Total Living Area	3,652 sq. ft.

PRICE CODE: F

CUSTOMIZE IT!

ORDER TOLL FREE 1■800■533■4350   **24-HOUR FAX ORDERING** 1■800■344■4293

201

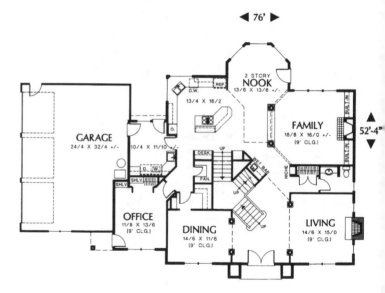

First Floor   2,150 sq. ft.
Second Floor   1,512 sq. ft.
Total Living Area   3,662 sq. ft.

PRICE CODE: D

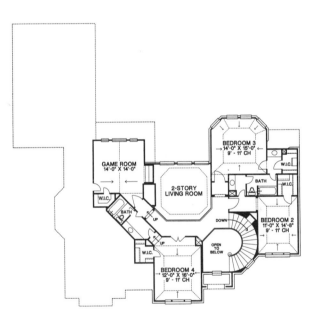

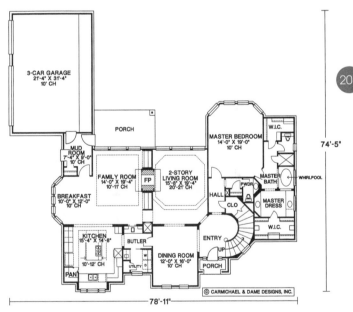

First Floor	2,321 sq. ft.
Second Floor	1,356 sq. ft.
Total Living Area	3,677 sq. ft.

PRICE CODE: F

204

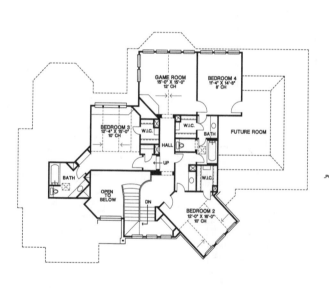

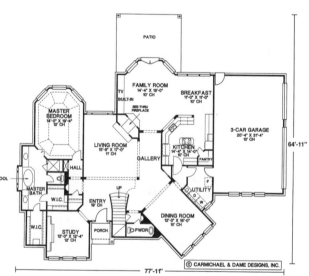

© CARMICHAEL & DAME DESIGNS, INC.

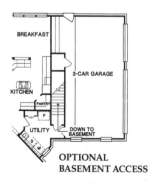

OPTIONAL
BASEMENT ACCESS

First Floor	2,362 sq. ft.
Second Floor	1,319 sq. ft.
Total Living Area	3,681 sq. ft.

PRICE CODE: F

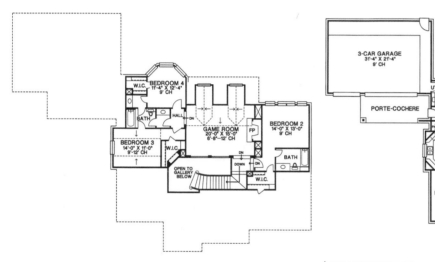

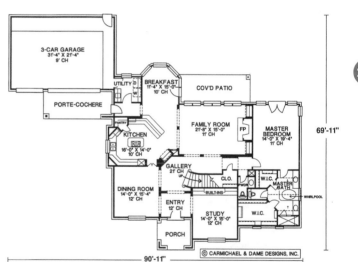

205

BEDROOM 4
11'-4" X 12'-4"
9' CH

W.I.C.

BATH

HALL

DN

GAME ROOM
20'-0" X 15'-0"
6'-8"-12' CH

FP

BEDROOM 2
14'-0" X 13'-0"
9' CH

W.I.C.

BEDROOM 3
14'-0" X 11'-0"
9'-12' CH

DN

DOWN

DN

BATH

OPEN TO GALLERY BELOW

W.I.C.

3-CAR GARAGE
31'-4" X 21'-4"
9' CH

UTILITY

BREAKFAST
11'-4" X 15'-0"
10' CH

COV'D PATIO

PORTE-COCHERE

PANTRY

KITCHEN
16'-0" X 14'-0"
10' CH

FAMILY ROOM
21'-8" X 15'-0"
11' CH

FP

MASTER BEDROOM
14'-0" X 19'-4"
11' CH

69'-11"

GALLERY
21' CH

CLO.

W.I.C.

MASTER BATH

WHIRLPOOL

DINING ROOM
14'-0" X 15'-4"
12' CH

BUILT-INS

PWDR

ENTRY
12' CH

STUDY
14'-0" X 15'-0"
12' CH

W.I.C.

PORCH

© CARMICHAEL & DAME DESIGNS, INC.

90'-11"

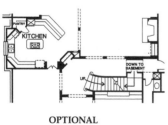

PANTRY

KITCHEN

DOWN TO BASEMENT

UP

**OPTIONAL
BASEMENT ACCESS**

First Floor	**2,350 sq. ft.**
Second Floor	**1,378 sq. ft.**
Total Living Area	**3,728 sq. ft.**

PRICE CODE: F

GALLERY

UTILITY

PWDR

DOWN TO BASEMENT

**OPTIONAL
BASEMENT ACCESS**

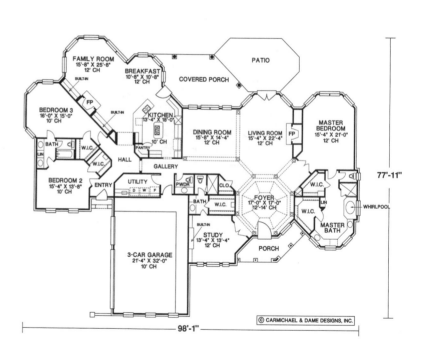

Total Living Area   3,734 sq. ft

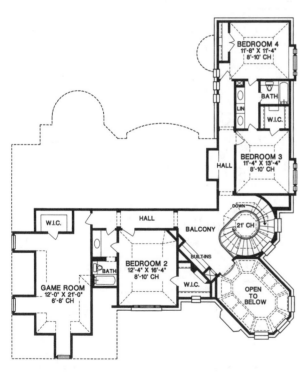

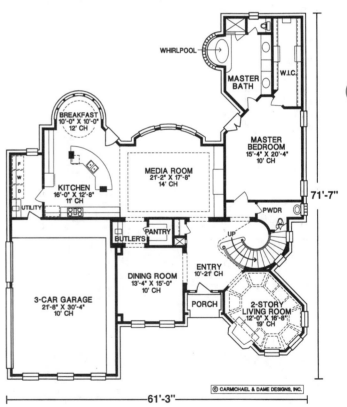

207

BEDROOM 4
11'-8" X 11'-4"
8'-10' CH

BATH

LIN

W.I.C.

HALL

BEDROOM 3
11'-4" X 13'-4"
8'-10' CH

DOWN
21' CH

BALCONY

BUILT-INS

W.I.C.

HALL

W.I.C.

BATH

BEDROOM 2
12'-4" X 16'-4"
8'-10' CH

GAME ROOM
12'-0" X 21'-0"
6'-8" CH

OPEN
TO
BELOW

WHIRLPOOL

MASTER BATH

W.I.C.

MASTER BEDROOM
15'-4" X 20'-4"
10' CH

BREAKFAST
10'-0" X 10'-0"
12' CH

F W D

MEDIA ROOM
21'-2" X 17'-8"
14' CH

KITCHEN
16'-0" X 12'-8"
11' CH

UTILITY

PWDR

BUTLER'S

PANTRY

UP

ENTRY
10'-21' CH

3-CAR GARAGE
21'-8" X 30'-4"
10' CH

DINING ROOM
13'-4" X 15'-0"
10' CH

PORCH

2-STORY LIVING ROOM
12'-0" X 16'-8"
19' CH

71'-7"

61'-3"

© CARMICHAEL & DAME DESIGNS, INC.

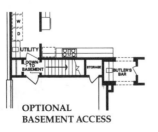

W D

UTILITY

DOWN TO BASEMENT

STORAGE

BUTLER'S BAR

OPTIONAL BASEMENT ACCESS

First Floor	2,199 sq. ft.
Second Floor	1,551 sq. ft.
Total Living Area	3,750 sq. ft.

PRICE CODE: F

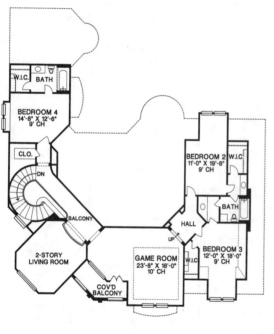

BEDROOM 4
14'-8" X 12'-6"
9' CH

W.I.C.   BATH

CLO.

DN

BALCONY

2-STORY
LIVING ROOM

COV'D
BALCONY

BEDROOM 2
11'-0" X 19'-8"
9' CH   W.I.C.

HALL

UP

BATH

GAME ROOM
23'-8" X 18'-0"
10' CH

W.I.C.

BEDROOM 3
12'-0" X 18'-0"
9' CH

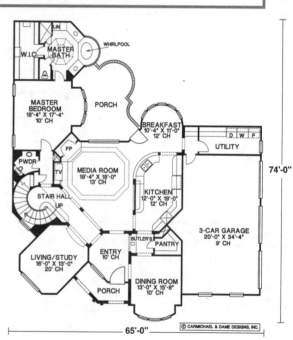

LIN

W.I.C.   MASTER
BATH   WHIRLPOOL

MASTER
BEDROOM
18'-4" X 17'-4"
10' CH   PORCH

BREAKFAST
10'-4" X 11'-0"
12' CH   D W F

UTILITY

PWDR   FP

TV

MEDIA ROOM
19'-4" X 18'-0"
13' CH

KITCHEN
12'-0" X 19'-0"
12' CH

STAIR HALL   UP

3-CAR GARAGE
20'-0" X 34'-4"
9' CH

BUTLER'S   PANTRY

LIVING/STUDY
16'-0" X 13'-0"
20' CH   ENTRY
10' CH

PORCH

DINING ROOM
13'-0" X 15'-8"
10' CH

© CARMICHAEL & DAME DESIGNS, INC.

74'-0"

65'-0"

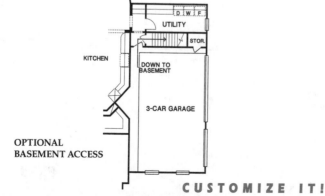

D W F

UTILITY

STOR.

KITCHEN

DOWN TO
BASEMENT

3-CAR GARAGE

OPTIONAL
BASEMENT ACCESS

First Floor	2,301 sq. ft.
Second Floor	1,473 sq. ft.
Total Living Area	3,774 sq. ft.

PRICE CODE: F

CUSTOMIZE IT!

ORDER TOLL FREE 1■800■533■4350   **24-HOUR FAX ORDERING** 1■800■344■4293

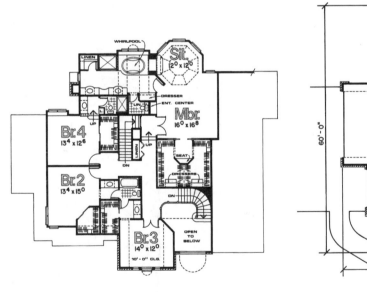

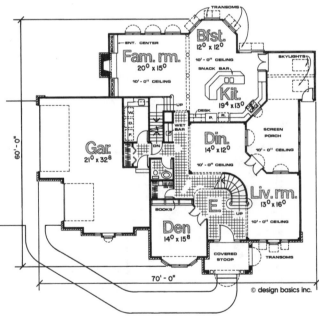

209

© design basics inc.

Features

- Living room has arched view into screen porch and decorative curved wall.
- Large kitchen with bayed dinette, huge island sink area with raised snack bar, desk and wrapping counters.
- Bedrooms #2 and #3 with walk-in closets share a roomy Hollywood bath.
- Bedroom #4 has private bath and walk-in closet.

- Master bath has walk-in linen storage, glass block wall, whirlpool and his and her vanities with make-up area.
- Sumptuous master suite with see-thru fireplace between sitting room and whirlpool, entertainment center, three built-in dressers and magnificent his and her walk-in closets.

First Floor	1,923 sq. ft.
Second Floor	1,852 sq. ft.
Total Living Area	3,775 sq. ft.

PRICE CODE: E

CUSTOMIZE IT!

ORDER TOLL FREE 1■800■533■4350   24-HOUR FAX ORDERING 1■800■344■4293

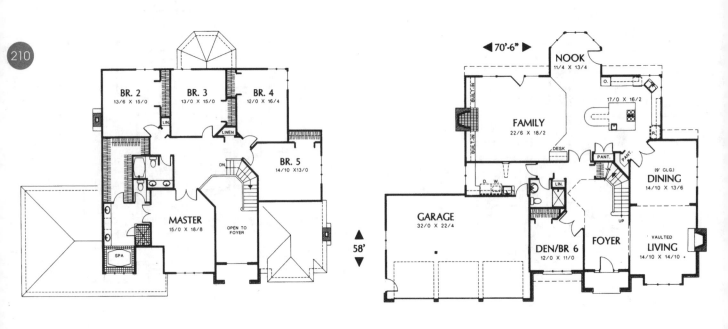

First Floor — 2,020 sq. ft.
Second Floor — 1,784 sq. ft.
Total Living Area — 3,804 sq. ft.

PRICE CODE: D

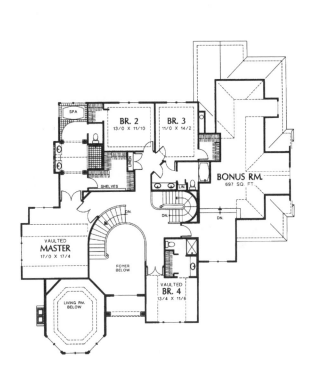

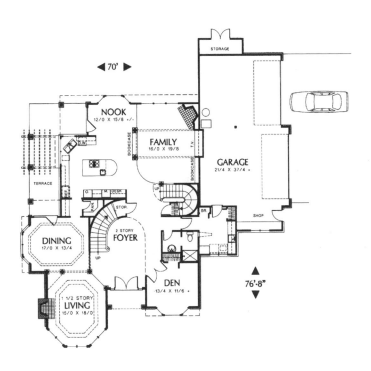

First Floor	2,190 sq. ft.
Second Floor	1,680 sq. ft.
Total Living Area	3,870 sq. ft.
Bonus Room	+697 sq. ft.

PRICE CODE: F

CUSTOMIZE IT!

ORDER TOLL FREE 1 ▪ 800 ▪ 533 ▪ 4350   24-HOUR FAX ORDERING   1 ▪ 800 ▪ 344 ▪ 4293

PLAN CD9156

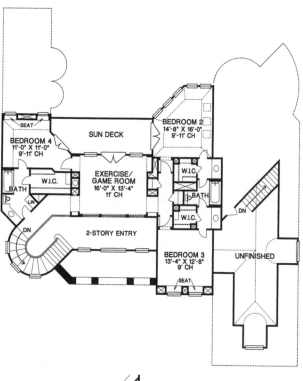

Second floor plan labels:
- SEAT
- BEDROOM 4 11'-0" X 11'-0" 9'-11" CH
- SUN DECK
- BEDROOM 2 14'-8" X 16'-0" 9'-11" CH
- BATH
- W.I.C.
- LIN
- EXERCISE/ GAME ROOM 16'-0" X 13'-4" 11' CH
- W.I.C.
- BATH
- W.I.C.
- DN
- DN
- 2-STORY ENTRY
- BEDROOM 3 13'-4" X 12'-8" 9' CH
- UNFINISHED
- SEAT

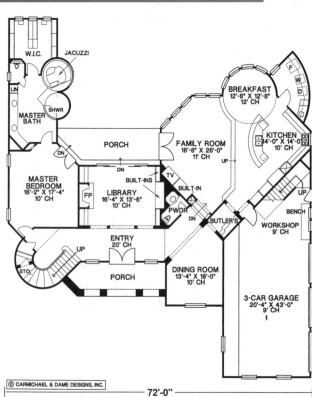

First floor plan labels:
- W.I.C.
- JACUZZI
- BREAKFAST 12'-8" X 12'-8" 12' CH
- LIN
- SHWR
- KITCHEN 14'-0" X 14'-0" 10' CH
- MASTER BATH
- PORCH
- FAMILY ROOM 16'-8" X 26'-0" 11' CH
- DN
- UP
- MASTER BEDROOM 16'-2" X 17'-4" 10' CH
- FP
- TV
- BUILT-INS
- BUILT-IN
- LIBRARY 16'-4" X 13'-6" 10' CH
- PWDR
- BENCH
- WORKSHOP 9' CH
- UP
- DN
- BUTLER'S
- ENTRY 20' CH
- UP
- STO
- PORCH
- DINING ROOM 13'-4" X 18'-0" 10' CH
- 3-CAR GARAGE 20'-4" X 43'-0" 9' CH

© CARMICHAEL & DAME DESIGNS, INC.

72'-0"

Optional basement access diagram:
- BUTLER'S
- UP
- DOWN TO BASEMENT
- WORKSHOP
- GARAGE

OPTIONAL BASEMENT ACCESS

First Floor	2,562 sq. ft.
Second Floor	1,332 sq. ft.
Total Living Area	3,894 sq. ft.

PRICE CODE: F

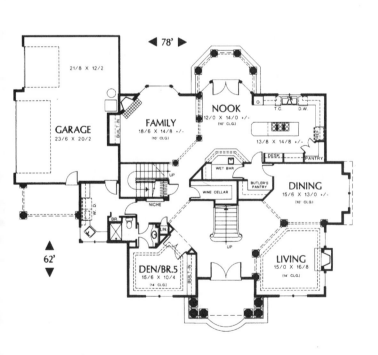

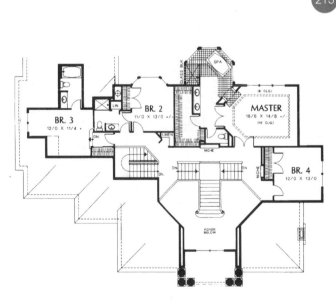

First Floor	2,342 sq. ft.
Second Floor	1,597 sq. ft.
Total Living Area	3,939 sq. ft.

PRICE CODE: F

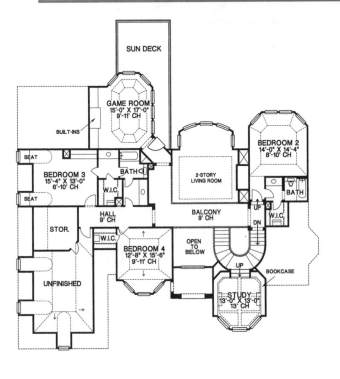

SUN DECK

GAME ROOM
15'-4" X 17'-0"
8'-11" CH

BUILT-INS

BEDROOM 2
14'-0" X 14'-4"
8'-10" CH

SEAT

BEDROOM 3
15'-4" X 13'-0"
6'-10" CH

BATH

W.I.C.

2-STORY
LIVING ROOM

SEAT

BATH

HALL
9' CH

STOR.

W.I.C.

BALCONY
9' CH

UP

W.I.C.

DN

BEDROOM 4
12'-8" X 15'-6"
9'-11" CH

OPEN
TO
BELOW

UNFINISHED

UP

STUDY
13'-0" X 13'-0"
13' CH

BOOKCASE

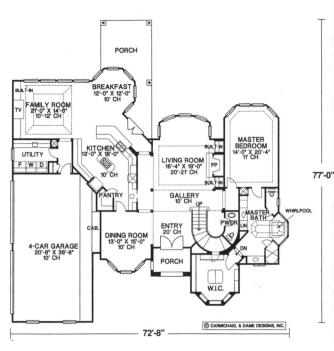

PORCH

BREAKFAST
12'-0" X 12'-0"
10' CH

BUILT-IN

FAMILY ROOM
21'-0" X 14'-0"
10'-12' CH

TV

UTILITY

F W D

KITCHEN
13'-0" X 18'-0"
10' CH

LIVING ROOM
16'-4" X 19'-0"
20'-21' CH

BUILT-IN

FP

MASTER
BEDROOM
14'-0" X 20'-4"
11' CH

BUILT-IN

PANTRY

GALLERY
10' CH

UP

WHIRLPOOL

4-CAR GARAGE
20'-8" X 36'-8"
10' CH

CAB.

DINING ROOM
13'-0" X 15'-0"
10' CH

ENTRY
20' CH

PWDR

LIN

MASTER
BATH

PORCH

DN

W.I.C.

© CARMICHAEL & DAME DESIGNS, INC.

77'-0"

72'-8"

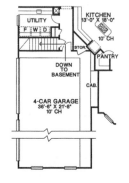

UTILITY

F W D

KITCHEN
13'-0" X 18'-0"
10' CH

STOR.

PANTRY

DOWN
TO
BASEMENT

CAB.

4-CAR GARAGE
36'-6" X 21'-8"
10' CH

First Floor	2,489 sq. ft.
Second Floor	1,650 sq. ft.
Total Living Area	4,139 sq. ft.

PRICE CODE: F

215

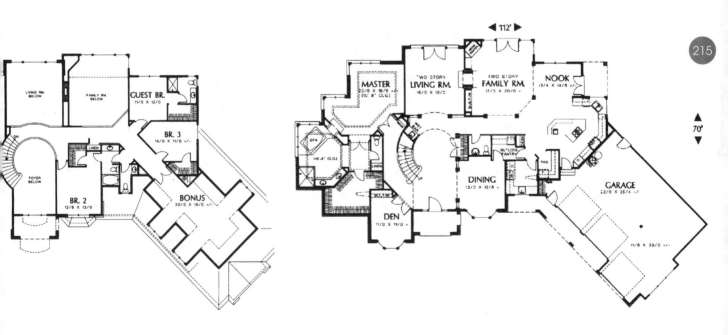

◀ 112' ▶

MASTER
20/8 x 18/6
(10'-8" CLG.)

TWO STORY
LIVING RM.
16/0 x 18/0

TWO STORY
FAMILY RM.
17/0 x 20/0 +/-

NOOK
13/4 x 14/8 +/-

SPA
(16'-8" CLG.)

LINEN

BUTLERS
PANTRY

PAN.

70'

DINING
13/0 x 12/8 +/-

GARAGE
22/0 x 26/4 +/-

DEN
11/0 x 11/0

11/8 x 30/0 +/-

LIVING RM.
BELOW

FAMILY RM.
BELOW

GUEST BR.
11/0 x 12/0

BR. 3
14/0 x 11/0 +/-

DN.

LINEN

FOYER
BELOW

BR. 2
12/8 x 13/0

BONUS
30/0 x 15/0 +/-

First Floor	3,098 sq. ft.
Second Floor	1,113 sq. ft.
Total Living Area	4,211 sq. ft.
Bonus Room	+567 sq. ft.

PRICE CODE: F

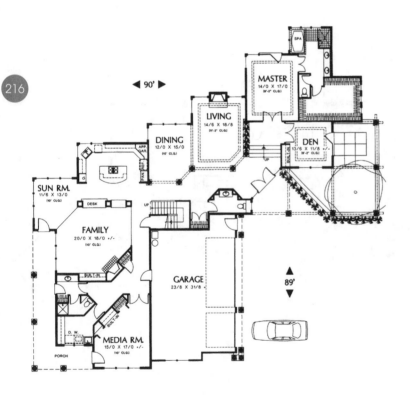

◀ 90' ▶

MASTER
14/0 X 17/0
(9'-2" CLG.)

LIVING
14/6 X 18/8
(9'-2" CLG.)

DINING
12/0 X 15/0
(10' CLG.)

DEN
13/6 X 11/8
(9'-2" CLG.)

SUN RM.
11/6 X 13/0
(10' CLG.)

FAMILY
20/0 X 18/0 +/-
(10' CLG.)

GARAGE
23/8 X 31/8

MEDIA RM.
15/0 X 17/0 +/-
(10' CLG.)

PORCH

▲
89'
▼

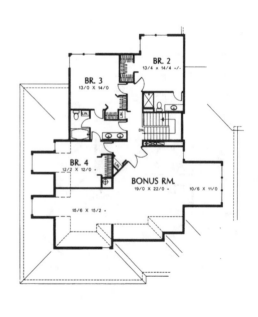

BR. 2
13/4 x 14/4 +/-

BR. 3
13/0 X 14/0

BR. 4
12/2 X 12/0

BONUS RM.
19/0 X 22/0 +
10/6 X 11/0

15/6 X 15/2 +

First Floor	3,258 sq. ft.
Second Floor	968 sq. ft.
Total Living Area	4,226 sq. ft.
Bonus Room	+858 sq. ft.

PRICE CODE: F

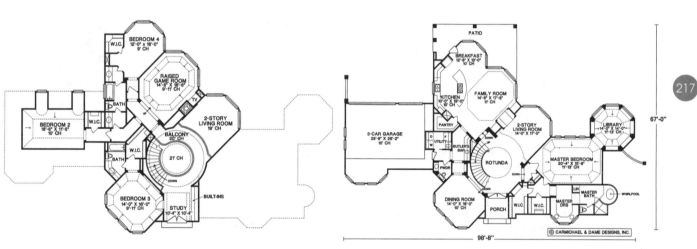

217

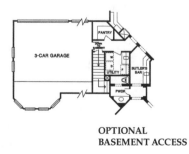

**OPTIONAL
BASEMENT ACCESS**

First Floor	2,551 sq. ft.
Second Floor	1,709 sq. ft.
Total Living Area	4,260 sq. ft.

PRICE CODE: F

CUSTOMIZE IT!

ORDER TOLL FREE 1▪800▪533▪4350 **24-HOUR FAX ORDERING** 1▪800▪344▪4293

PLAN CD9153

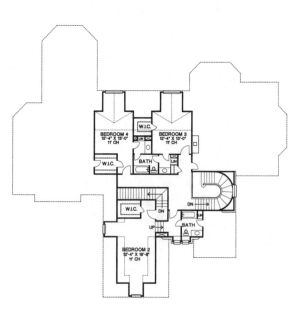

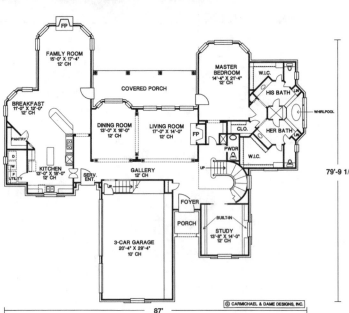

218

GALLERY
12' CH

DOWN TO BASEMENT

**OPTIONAL
BASEMENT ACCESS**

87'

79'-9 1/2"

© CARMICHAEL & DAME DESIGNS, INC.

First Floor	3,026 sq. ft.
Second Floor	1,377 sq. ft.
Total Living Area	4,403 sq. ft.

PRICE CODE: F

CUSTOMIZE IT!

ORDER TOLL FREE 1■800■533■4350   24-HOUR FAX ORDERING   1■800■344■4293

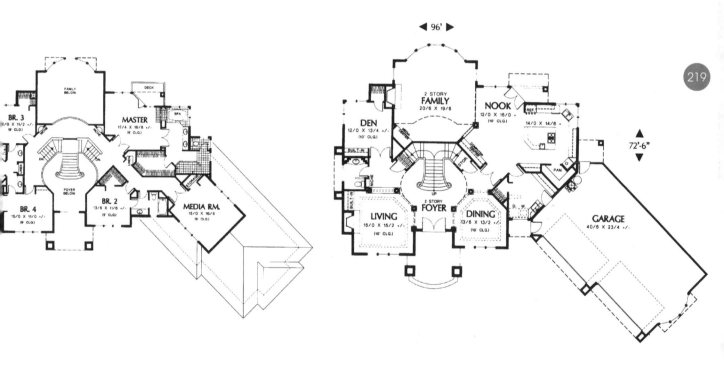

219

First Floor 2,290 sq. ft.
Second Floor 2,142 sq. ft.
Total Living Area 4,432 sq. ft.

PRICE CODE: F

220

OPTIONAL
BASEMENT ACCESS

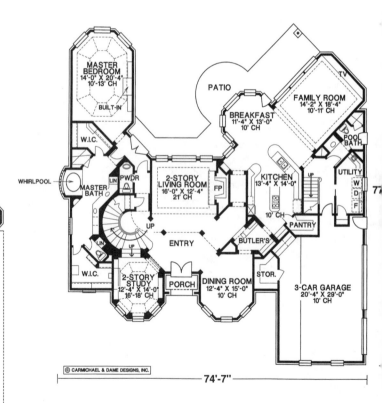

© CARMICHAEL & DAME DESIGNS, INC.

74'-7"

First Floor	2,897 sq. ft.
Second Floor	1,603 sq. ft.
Total Living Area	4,500 sq. ft.

PRICE CODE: F

PLAN CD9102

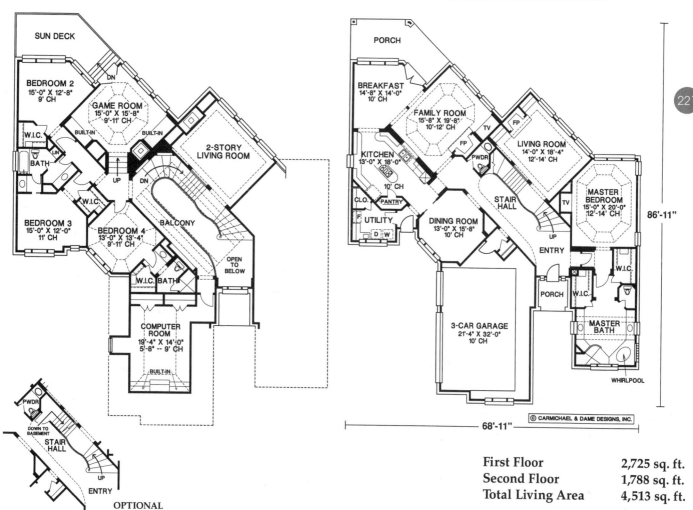

SUN DECK

BEDROOM 2
15'-0" X 12'-8"
9' CH

GAME ROOM
15'-0" X 15'-8"
9'-11' CH

DN

W.I.C.

BUILT-IN | BUILT-IN

UP

BATH

LIN

DN

2-STORY LIVING ROOM

W.I.C.

BEDROOM 3
15'-0" X 12'-0"
11' CH

BALCONY

BEDROOM 4
13'-0" X 13'-4"
9'-11' CH

W.I.C. BATH

OPEN TO BELOW

COMPUTER ROOM
19'-4" X 14'-0"
5'-8" -- 9' CH

BUILT-IN

PWDR

DOWN TO BASEMENT

STAIR HALL

UP

ENTRY

OPTIONAL BASEMENT ACCESS

PORCH

BREAKFAST
14'-8" X 14'-0"
10' CH

FAMILY ROOM
15'-8" X 19'-8"
10'-12' CH

TV | FP

FP

KITCHEN
13'-0" X 18'-0"
10' CH

LIVING ROOM
14'-0" X 18'-4"
12'-14' CH

PWDR

FP

CLO.

PANTRY

STAIR HALL

TV

MASTER BEDROOM
15'-0" X 20'-0"
12'-14' CH

F

UTILITY

D | W

DINING ROOM
13'-0" X 15'-8"
10' CH

UP

ENTRY

W.I.C.

PORCH | W.I.C.

3-CAR GARAGE
21'-4" X 32'-0"
10' CH

MASTER BATH

WHIRLPOOL

© CARMICHAEL & DAME DESIGNS, INC.

86'-11"

68'-11"

221

First Floor 2,725 sq. ft.
Second Floor 1,788 sq. ft.
Total Living Area 4,513 sq. ft.

PRICE CODE: F

81'8(24.9m)

222

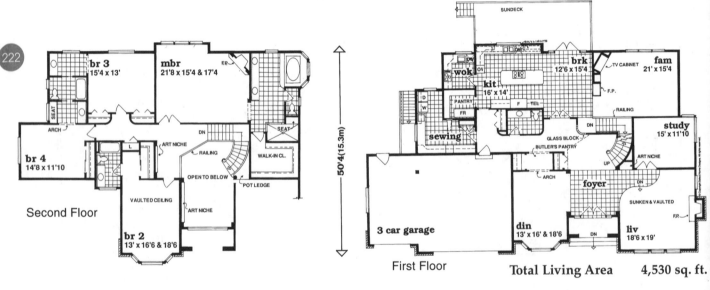

br 3
15'4 x 13'

mbr
21'8 x 15'4 & 17'4

F.R.

SEAT

ARCH

br 4
14'8 x 11'10

L

ART NICHE

DN

RAILING

SEAT

WALK-IN CL.

OPEN TO BELOW

POT LEDGE

Second Floor

VAULTED CEILING

ART NICHE

br 2
13' x 16'6 & 18'6

50'4(15.3m)

SUNDECK

SKYLIGHTS

DW   OV

wok   OV

kit
16' x 14'

brk
12'6 x 15'4

TV CABINET

fam
21' x 15'4

F.P.

D

W

FR

PANTRY

F   TEL

RAILING

DN

sewing

GLASS BLOCK

BUTLER'S PANTRY

study
15' x 11'10

ARCH

UP

ART NICHE

foyer

DN

3 car garage

din
13' x 16' & 18'6

DN

SUNKEN & VAULTED

F.P.

liv
18'6 x 19'

First Floor

Total Living Area   4,530 sq. ft.

media rm
23' x 12'4 & 14'4

FIREPLACE

games rm
33'2 x 15'2

FURNACE   HWT   HRV

WET BAR

mud rm   mech

brm5
14'4 x 11'

UP

ART NICHE

storage

ART NICHE

exercise
17'8 x 16'4

Basement

Features

- Curved staircase greets dramatic foyer.
- Main floor includes convenient amenities such as a sewing room, a separate wok kitchen and a butler's pantry.
- Kitchen boasts a walk-in pantry, expansive counter space and an island kitchen with a built-in stove.
- Master bedroom hosts a dramatic double-door with a large ensuite.

PRICE CODE: F

CUSTOMIZE IT!

ORDER TOLL FREE   **1■800■533■4350**   **24-HOUR FAX ORDERING**   **1■800■344■4293**

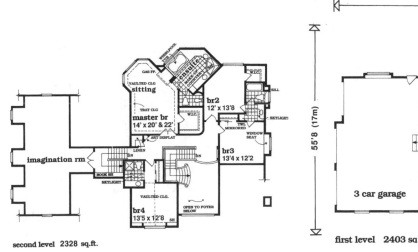

second level 2328 sq.ft.

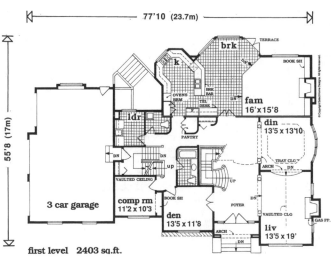

first level 2403 sq.ft.

Features

- Sunken living room's curved window mirrors the archway to the dining room and accentuates the vaulted ceiling.
- Dining room boasts a tray ceiling and elegant bay window.
- Den or in-home office has a convenient access to a full three-piece bathroom.
- Gourmet kitchen with expansive bay of counter and cupboards features a pantry, raised eating bar for counter-top meals, desk and sunny breakfast room.
- Master bedroom boasts a bay window sitting area and see-through fireplace.
- Sumptuous ensuite offers his and hers vanity, oversized plan shower, spacious walk-in closet and separate bidet and toilet room.

First Floor	2,403 sq. ft.
Second Floor	2,328 sq. ft.
Total Living Area	4,731 sq. ft.

PRICE CODE: F

CUSTOMIZE IT!

ORDER TOLL FREE 1∎800∎533∎4350   24-HOUR FAX ORDERING 1∎800∎344∎4293

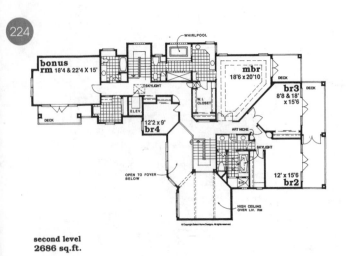

second level
2686 sq.ft.

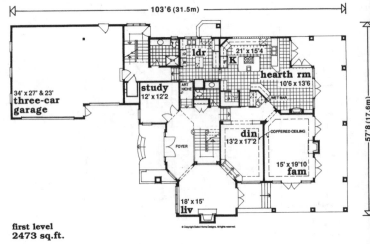

first level
2473 sq.ft.

Features

- Volume ceiling extending from the entry foyer to the living room is accentuated by multi-paned transom windows and open staircase.
- Butler's pantry with stemware plan shelves, wet bar, fridge and microwave eases service to the dining room from the gourmet kitchen.
- Kitchen boasts a walk-in pantry, wine cooler, built-in desk, expansive counter space and centre preparation island with cooktop and salad sink.

- Coffered ceiling family room with built-in media centre over the fireplace is surrounded by French doors.
- Bedrooms two and three, each with French door access to the covered deck, share a skylit bathroom with twin vanity, whirlpool spa and shower.

First Floor	2,473 sq. ft
Second Floor	2,686 sq. ft
Total Living Area	5,159 sq. ft

PRICE CODE: F